SYRUP TREES

By
Bruce
Thompson

The engraving on page 76 is from John C. van Tramp, *Life in the West,* 1863, Gilmore and Brush, Columbus, Ohio. The photos on page 87 and throughout Chapter 10 are courtesy of the photographer, Dick Smith.

Cover design by Julia Shea

Copyright © 1978 By Bruce Thompson
For further information write:
   Walnut Press
   P.O. Box 17210
   Fountain Hills, Arizona 85268
Printed in the United States of America by Imperial Litho/Graphics
Library of Congress Catalog Card Number 78-63316
ISBN 0-931318-00-9

Library of Congress Cataloging in Publication Data

Thompson, Bruce S
   Syrup trees.

   Bibliography: p.
   Includes index.
   1. Maple. 2. Sugar-maple. 3. Maple syrup.
   4. Cookery (Maple sugar and syrup) I. Title.
SB239.M3T46   633'.64   78-63316
ISBN 0-931318-00-9

Dedicated
With Love
to
My Wife
Louise

Contents

Foreword

Pressures against the traditional family farm are many and of diverse nature. The skills required for operation of a small farm dealing with numerous crops are rapidly being lost and will be difficult to recover.

The country village which at one time contained the grist- and saw mills, foundries, blacksmith shops and feed stores are now somnolent or catering to the tourists.

It is not possible to say that these changes are necessarily undesirable. It does seem to be true that the social and moral values which were held most closely in rural areas no doubt derived from the tightly-knit family and community.

What of the future? The changes which have occurred in agriculture and rural areas have the same basis as so many changes in all parts of our country—cheap fossil fuels. We may be entering a period when return to some less energy-intensive modes of living will be mandatory. The family farm and rural villages may be due for re-discovery. The young people who now want to get into agriculture usually find the costs prohibitive. Perhaps changing times will make it possible to put this future resource on the land.

An integral part of most family farms was the woodlot. From these came the fuel, some saw logs or pulp to be sold, and, where possible, maple syrup. The maple crop often paid the taxes or bought the fertilizer for crops.

This book points the way to some of the information on "sugaring" as we call it in Vermont, where *the* sugar maple grow and *the* maple syrup is produced. As with so many of the "arts," some of the necessary knowledge can only be found in the woods or over an evaporator.

There seems to be something about sugaring which enlarges the perception beyond the reality. It must be experienced to be understood.

Welcome to sugaring for those of you who will be influenced by this book!

Frederick M. Laing
Department of Botany
The University of Vermont

Preface

I don't think that it makes much difference why, but a goodly number of us would rather do it our way than do what is conventional and profitable. We enjoy life. We are told that we are too optimistic for our own good. We trust people. Somewhere along the line we have become convinced that our peace on earth, and our justification for being, come from leaving the little area where we work just a trifle better than we found it.

An assortment of current phrases such as "Back to Naturalness, Voluntary Simplicity, Turning to Basic Values, and Quality of Life" partially describe some of the common denominators imprinted upon us and distinguishing *us,* from *them.*

This leads to an infinite variety of wonderful options of things to do that are pleasant, unharmful to nature, and generally very inexpensive. There are painters, bird watchers, woodworkers, gardeners, historians, biologists, whalesavers, hummingbird feeders and house cleaners. All of them, in their individual way, keep "things" neat and respectable and livable, and all the while take a modest pride in their contribution.

Occasionally, however, the routine wears a bit thin and, subconsciously perhaps, we ask for, hope for, a trifle of recognition. It may be long in coming in most instances but not, I found, in the minor spring rite of tapping maple trees for their sap and syrup and sugar. Every local paper where tapping is done carries numerous photographs and articles on its own celebrities, who then assume the enviable and equivalent status of the crocus or the first robin of spring. "How to," plus suggestions for a serious, full-time occupation, is the purpose of this book. Hopefully it will permit you to see the opportunities at your own doorstep and the many others nearby.

Acknowledgments

When Helen and Scott Nearing declined to publish an updated version of their 1950 edition of *The Maple Sugar Book,* I assumed the assignment with an innocence unbecoming my years.

Thanks to the wholehearted cooperation and assistance of numerous experts and authorities, however, this current picture of the maple syrup/sugar art was made possible. They include:

Dr. F. Bryan Clark, Director, Northeastern Forest Experiment Station, 370 Reed Road, Broomall, Pennsylvania 19008

Neil K. Huyler, Forest Products Technologist, Northeastern Forest Experiment Station, Burlington, Vermont

Dr. Lloyd H. Sipple, Publisher, *National Maple Syrup Digest,* Bainbridge, New York

Dr. Melvin R. Koelling, Michigan State University, East Lansing, Michigan

Mr. Lewis Staats, Regional Extension Specialist, Lake
Placid, New York

William F. Cowen, Jr., Extension Forester, Columbus,
Ohio

Mr. Juan Reynolds, Reynolds Sugar Bush, Aniwa,
Wisconsin

Dr. Frederick M. Laing, University of Vermont, Burlington, Vermont

I am grateful, as are the people who have been making
maple syrup for years, for the numerous publications of Robert
R. Morrow, Cornell University, Ithica, New York. Though
somewhat technical, Agricultural Handbook No. 134 by C. O.
Willits and Claude H. Hills is the great reference and starting
point for any serious inquiry into this multifaceted industry.

My friends Jo Stipp of Forest City, Iowa and Imogene
Clarke of Harbor Springs, Michigan kindly provided photographs of this year's "sugarin'" operations in their localities.

1

Sugar Trees

Any serious published inquiry often reveals more than anticipated, and occasionally a startling revelation brings down upon
the investigator the curses, wrath, opprobrium and vitu-
peration of the establishment. My head is bowed, but the fact is
that the box elder tree is *Acer negundo,* a true and legitimate
member of the genus *Acer* of the family *Aceraceae.* The lofty
and regal sugar maple, *Acer saccharum,* praised in song and
story, the darling of poets and purists, the heart of Vermont,
and the glory of fall, will have to acknowledge its kinship with
this weak, unsightly, bug-harboring relative. Both yield pure
maple syrup, and that's what this inquiry is all about—where it
comes from, what we do with it, be it sugar maple, black maple,
silver maple, red maple or box elder.

Taylor's *Encyclopedia of Gardening* for 1948 states that
there are about 115 species of the genus *Acer,* while Scott
Leathart in his 1977 edition of *Trees of the World* reports over
200 species. I doubt if more than a few of these species have
been tapped for syrup, but the authors of *Edible Wild Plants of*

Northeastern America* mention the tapping of buttonwood, birches, basswood, cottonwood, hickory and even the walnuts, with the sap evaporated for sugar. The practice hardly seems worthwhile, however, when there are so many fine maples readily at hand. Black walnut, for instance, will yield a substantial amount of sap, but the damage to the wood from the harvesting process makes this a very costly experiment.

Vermonters may think it heresy to so state, but there are sugar trees west to California and north to Alaska, as the following maps will show. Somewhat inferior though they may be to the grand *Acer saccharum* (the sugar maple of the Eastern U.S.) the western trees do deserve and undoubtedly will receive far more attention than they have in the past. With dark amber maple syrup retailing at health food and mail order stores for $6.59 to $7.50 a quart, they can hardly be ignored.

The early settlers in the Ohio Valley and eastward found *Acer saccharum* (sugar maple or hard maple) in great abundance, a joyful answer to their need for a sweetener. Over the years, producers of maple syrup and maple sugar have let it be known that sugar trees other than *Acer saccharum* yield about one-third less sap, that the sap was about one-third less sweet, and that it contained excessive amounts of minerals (sugar sand) to be filtered out before the syrup was useable. Newcomers and strangers were laughed at when they innocently tapped a red maple. Those seriously in the business removed the red and silver maples, and of course the box elders, maintaining that a contamination, an off-flavor, might result from mixing the sap. And in fact, expert syrup tasters—real connoisseurs—claim they can detect a pungent, slightly bitter aftertaste in syrup made from trees other than black or sugar maple.

Whatever the claims may be, the fact is that a Michigan producer I know has a silver maple whose sugar sap content is 6%, well above the national average for sugar maple. Furthermore, in northern Michigan in 1978 many producers reported needing 55 to 65 gallons of sap from *Acer saccharum* to make a single gallon of syrup, compared to the 40 gallons of box elder sap in northern Iowa used to make the same amount.

*Merritt Lynden Fernald and Alfred Charles Kinsey, 1958, *Edible Wild Plants of Eastern North America*, 4th ed., Harper and Row.

Not only that, but a taste comparison between Iowa box elder syrup and Wisconsin sugar maple syrup, both pure maple syrup—dark amber—gave the advantage to the Iowa product. It's true the test was highly unscientific and that the palates tested were jaded, dulled and insensitive after years of subjection to artificial foods and flavors, but that condition is nearly universal anyway.

In any event, only a tiny fraction of the sugar maple, and almost none of the other maples is being tapped now. So from coast to coast we all can have our weekend, our two months or our year of "maplin' " without fear of running short of trees.

The following maps showing the geographical distribution of some of the maples are taken from the *Atlas of United States Trees,* vol. 1, by Albert L. Little, Jr. (1971, Forest Service, Miscellaneous Publication No. 1146). There are occasional exceptions that warrant seeing trees as individuals rather than just looking at the woods. For example, I found a small stand of sugar maple 20 miles east of Payson, Arizona—a most unlikely spot.

The illustrations below from the *1949 Yearbook of Agriculture* show the leaf and the seed of six native maples you will be tapping. The papery, veiny-winged seeds are called samaras and are common also to elm, ash and basswood, though not joined, as with maples. The samaras of the red maple are the smallest, being about ¾ inch in length. Sugar and black maple samaras are about 1¼ inches long, box elder and big leaf about 1½ inches and silver maple about 1⅝ inches.

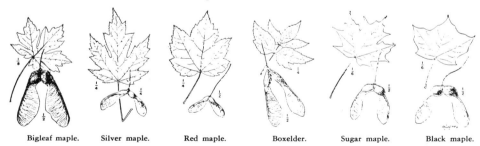

Bigleaf maple.   Silver maple.   Red maple.   Boxelder.   Sugar maple.   Black maple.

NOTE: An excellent map showing the general range of all trees in the United States, entitled "Forest Types—Sheet No. 182," is available for $1.50 from the U.S. Geological Survey, Washington, D.C. 20242.

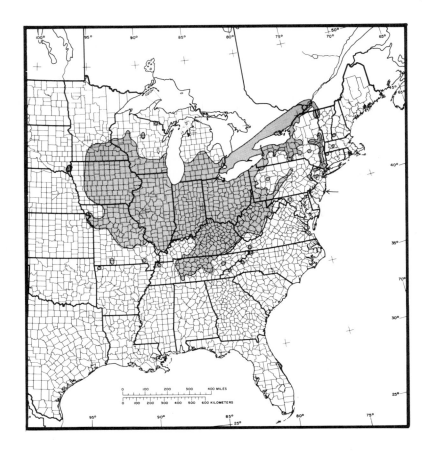

Acer saccharum—sugar maple, rock maple, hard maple

    This tree, the state tree of both Vermont and New York, produces the bulk of the maple syrup and sugar made in the U.S. and Canada. It grows rather slowly to a height of 60 to 120 feet, with a remarkably clean trunk in the forest or a beautiful, broad, round-topped dome when open-grown. It prefers

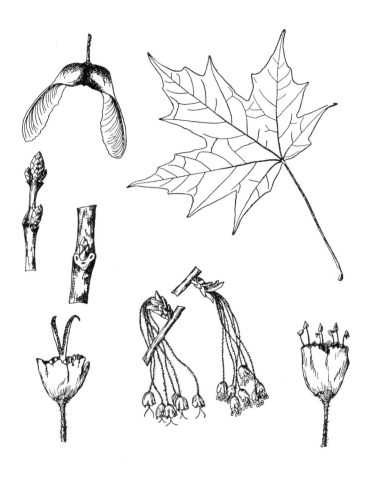

moist, rich soil in valleys and uplands and moist, rocky slopes. Its leaves turn a glorious yellow, orange, scarlet and red in the autumn. The wood is hard, strong, tough and heavy and has the distinction of being a perfect firewood. The leaves are dark green above, light green or pale and usually smooth beneath.

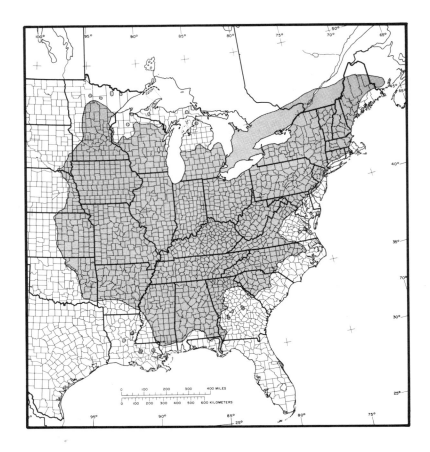

Acer saccharinum—silver maple, soft maple, white maple, river maple

    This is a large, rapid-growing tree which adapts itself to a wide variety of soils, though it does not do well on dry, elevated ground. It will reach a height of 60–80 or even 100 feet and is used for shade as well as in shelter belts. It is one of the first trees to blossom in the spring. Its leaves are light green above

and silvery white beneath, turning pale yellow in autumn. Though rather brittle and perishable, the wood is used in boxes, crates and less expensive furniture. There are also several varieties of silver maple known as cutleaf maple.

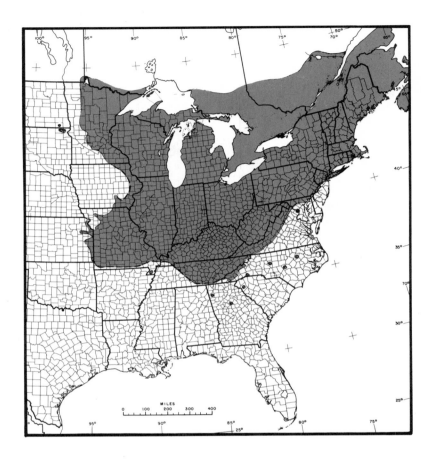

Acer nigrum—black maple, black sugar maple, sugar maple

 This maple resembles *Acer saccharum* in so many ways that it is often considered a variety of the sugar maple. Its distinguishing feature is its dense coating of velvety, brownish hairs on the under surface of the leaf and on the leaf stalk. The leaves have a flabby look with the edges hanging down, giving

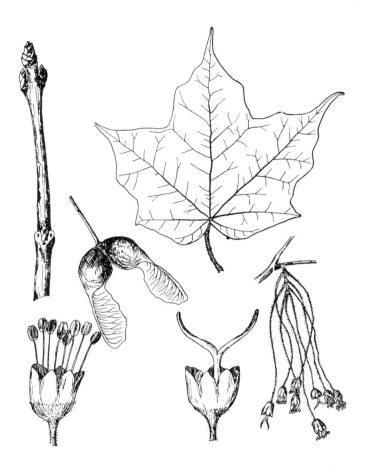

the tree an air of depression. They turn yellow in the fall. Some old timers claim that the finest grades of maple syrup are made from the sap of this tree. Like *Acer saccharum,* the lumber of the *Acer nigrum* makes excellent furniture, flooring, boxes, woodenware, novelties, etc.

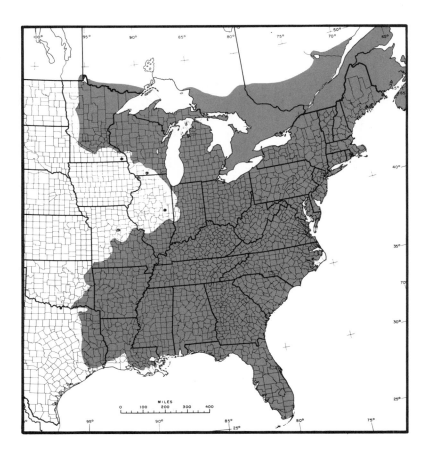

Acer rubrum—red maple, soft maple, scarlet maple

This medium-sized tree tends to grow 40–50 feet high, though on swamplands and banks of streams it may reach 75 feet or more. Its upright branches form a low, rather narrow, rounded crown. The leaves are paired, heart-shaped, 2½ to 4 inches long, dark green and shiny above, whitish and slightly hairy beneath, turning scarlet or yellow in the fall. The tree was

a favorite of Henry Thoreau. Like that of the silver maple, the red maple fruit matures very early in the summer when it drops and germinates. (Other maple seeds are not mature until autumn.) Maple syrup has been made from this tree in limited quantities for many years.

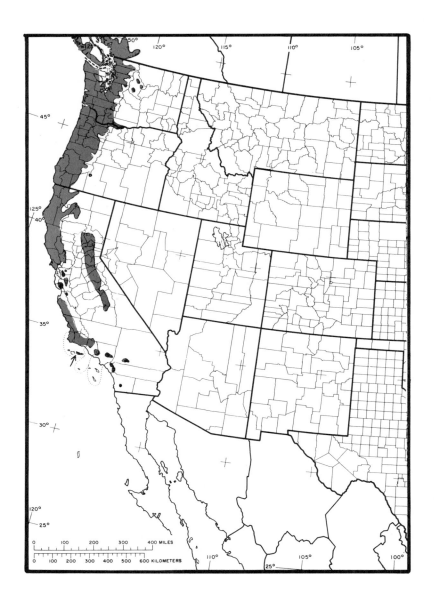

12　SYRUP TREES

Acer macrophullum—bigleaf maple, oregon maple, broadleaf maple

This large hardwood of the Pacific coast region ranges from California to Alaska. When open-grown, its trunk will grow to 2 or 3 or even 5 feet in diameter and attain a height of up to 100 feet. In competition with the Douglas fir within their natural range, these maples become spindly, though their bright yellow-orange foliage in the fall provides a beautiful contrast to the pines. The leaves are 8 to 10 inches wide and long, somewhat leathery at maturity and dark green above and pale below. The wood is weak, soft and light, but it does find many commercial uses. Donald Cutross Peattie writes in his book *A Natural History of Western Trees*, "Sugar has been made from the sap, and the nectar of the flowers is sought by honey bees."

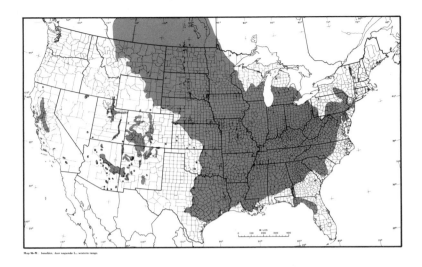

Map 96-W, boxelder, Acer negundo L., western range.

Acer negundo—box elder, ash-leaf maple, Manitoba maple, three-leaf maple

This sturdy little tree accommodates itself to almost any situation. It is fast growing but short lived. It tends to reach 30–50 feet in most locations, but when protected in a closed stand may go to 60–75 feet or more. The trunk often divides near the ground into several stout, wide-spreading branches, forming a broad asymetrical open crown. The wood is light, soft, close-grained and creamy white, with thick, hardly distinguishable sapwood. It makes a poor firewood, but its capability as a quick windbreak made it a favorite with early pioneer settlers west of the Mississippi.

The leaves of these trees are paired and compound, usually in groups of 3 or 5, rarely 7 or 9, with the leaflets 2½ to 4 inches long and 1½ to 2½ inches broad, light green above, paler and sometimes hairy on the veins of the lower surface. In the East the leaves in the fall tend to be a dull brown, but in the West they are sometimes a rich red, and a soft light yellow is not uncommon. Two varieties native to the West, *A. n. californicum* and *A. n. interius*, range from Alberta to Arizona.

In Charles A. Eastman's book *Indian Boyhood* is this quotation: "It was usual to make sugar from maples, but several

other trees were also tapped by the Indians. From the birch and ash was made a dark-colored sugar, with a somewhat bitter taste, which was used for medicinal purposes. The box-elder yielded a beautiful white sugar, whose only fault was there was never enough of it." Donald Cutross Peattie noted the groves that had been tapped at the Standing Rock Reservation in North Dakota. And in the January 1891 issue of *American Anthropology*, an article entitled "The Maple Amongst the Algonkian Tribes" tells us that the thirteenth month of the year was called by the Indians the "sugar month" because "in it they manufactured their sugar from the maple and box-elder trees." It would be interesting to find out what this hardy little tree really could do in the way of sap production if it were properly fertilized and watered and generally cared for.

NOTE: Drawn illustrations are from Charles Herbert Otis, 1915, *Michigan Trees,* 6 ed., The Regents of the University of Michigan. Photographed illustrations are from E. J. Zavits, 1973, *Hardwood Trees of Ontario,* Ministry of Natural Resources.

2

Sugar Bush Management

Over the years I've planted several hundred thousand shrubs and trees, and of them all, the 4,000 sugar maple *(Acer saccharum),* which I carefully planted on good land, watered, fertilized and pruned, have been the most expensive, frustrating and unrewarding. Conversely, I have dropped hundreds of box elder *(Acer negundo)* transplants into hastily-dug holes and forgotten them—and they grew like the weeds the hardbitten maple syrup purists consider them to be.

There has to be a limit to what any of us can afford in outlay of cash or time, so if you do have black or sugar maple, cherish them and count your blessings. They are extremely slow-growing, and for all their glorious beauty and sugar-producing capability, I'd hesitate to recommend that they be cultured from seedlings.

Most of us are good environmentalists and subscribe to "naturalness" and the "reverence for life" concept as far as other peoples' property or the public lands are concerned. It becomes quite another matter, however, once a conflict arises which directly affects us and ours. Maples tend to be thrifty, hardy, worry-free and disease and insect-resistant. However, the time may come when you are convinced that something must be done to save your trees from gross destruction, permanent injury and death. When the one or ten or twenty of your best and only trees are concerned, you're likely, in good conscience, to take measures you wouldn't generally approve of or advocate. Just do whatever is necessary to save your trees, but do be mindful of the consequences.

Your local forester and county extension directors should be consulted before you begin a campaign against insects, diseases, virus and other killers. The magazine *Western Fruit Grower* annually lists suppliers of approved herbicides, insecticides, antibiotics, adjuvants, fungicides, miticides, fumigants and nematicides, rodenticides and bird and deer repellants, as well as a host of other tree-related items. Whether you are "organic" or not, I believe that those who really care for their trees owe it to both the trees and themselves to learn all there is to learn about management alternatives. The more we know, the better our judgment. And besides, learning about trees, or even a single tree, opens up a beautiful world of endless pleasant inquiry and observation.

Though you may have only a few trees and no intention of taking syrup-making very seriously, I urge you to read three booklets. They are:

1. *Sugar Bush Management* by Robert R. Morrow (Information Bulletin 110, Mailing Room, Building 7, Research Park, Cornell University, Ithaca, New York 14853, 60¢ a copy);
2. *Sugar Bush Management for Maple Syrup Producers* by C. F. Coons (Information Branch, Ontario Ministry of Natural Resources, Parliament Buildings, Toronto, Ontario M7A 1W3);
3. *A Silvicultural Guide for Developing a Sugar Bush* by Kenneth F. Lancaster, Russell S. Walters, Frederick M. Laing, Raymond T. Foulds (Research Paper NE-286, Northeastern Forest Experiment Station, 370 Reed Road, Broomall, Pennsylvania 19008).

Very recent work by such researchers as Dr. F. M. Laing of the University of Vermont's botany department has shown that even with standard horticultural procedures "tappable" trees can be obtained within 20 to 30 years versus 40 to 80 years for wild trees, and that the sweetness of their sap can be nearly doubled. Far better results might be obtained with cloning, but foresters, unlike nurserymen and timbermen in the soft wood industry, are reluctant to experiment in the debatable field of genetic tampering.

Since foresters tend to deal with vast numbers of trees, they deemphasize the importance of pruning individual trees. I recommend that you shape your tree annually the way you want it to grow. It will respond. At the same time remove dead and judiciously-selected undesired limbs. Your library will have various books on pruning techniques, perhaps including mine on pruning procedures for black walnut.

No maple trees I know of receive optimum amounts of fertilizer and water. Feeding procedures are difficult and expensive, but they may be worth the time and effort of experimentation. The standard for the highly productive fruit and nut crop trees of the west is to apply fertilizer through irrigation water. Possibly, and as a suggestion only, producers who are installing miles of plastic tubing for sap collection can use this same tubing for an improvised drip irrigation system.

Besides the diseases and insects mentioned in the booklets listed, the box elder tree also attracts the box elder bug, *Leptocoris trivittatus*. This is a minor blackish pest with red markings which sometimes enters houses and other sheltered places in the fall in search of hibernating quarters. The box elder bugs will not do any damage. But there are thousands upon thousands of different kinds of bugs and strains of diseases that can appear and destroy your trees without warning, and it is wise to know your state and university entomologists. These men not only know the availability of biological control material, but can aid you in "calling out the troops," whoever or whatever they may be. Although the locust and the chestnut and the elms disappeared from our countryside relatively slowly, a blight would have wiped out my black walnut seedlings within a week but for the assistance of Dr. Abe Epstein at Iowa State University.

One of the anomalies of our society is that the government often pays us to do things we were going to do anyway. Accordingly, contact your local Soil Conservation Service Office and the Agricultural Stabilization and Conservation Commission within the Department of Agriculture. Their helpful people will advise you on the current "practices" for which you are entitled to payment. They also administer the Forestry Incentives Program, which is available in many counties. These agencies have a long history of being helpful to fellow operators like you and me.

3

Equipment and Supplies

Roy and Jean Hanson of Joice, Iowa, made all of the equipment needed for their maple syrup bonanza, including elderberry spigots hollowed out with No. 9 wire. Not being that clever and ingenious myself, I wrote to a few regular suppliers for their catalogues of handy things to have for this rather out-of-the-ordinary pursuit. I thought you might enjoy seeing a reproduction of one, from Reynolds Sugar Bush Co. Print reproduction has impaired the catalogue's legibility somewhat, but it illustrates the wide range of potentially-useful items available. I have absolutely no personal interest in the firm, and neither do I necessarily recommend, endorse or guarantee any of its products.

Other old-line companies with excellent catalogues include:

G. H. Grimm Company, Pine Street, Rutland, Vermont
    05701 (802-775-5411)
Leader Evaporator Co., Inc., 25 Stowell Street, St. Albans,
    Vermont 05478 (802-524-3931)

Robert M. Lamb, Maple Sap Plastic Tube Gathering System, P.O. Box 368, Rt. 49, Bernhards Bay, New York 13028 (315-675-3652)

The National Maple Syrup Digest, Bainbridge, New York 13733 (carries ads from many suppliers)

Forestry Suppliers, Inc., 205 West Ranking Street, Jackson, Mississippi 39204 (601-354-3565) (does *not* supply maple related products, but lists hundreds of useful forestry related items)

REYNOLDS SUGAR BUSH

PHONE (A.C. 715) 449-2057 or 449-2536
ANIWA, WISCONSIN 54408

Use the enclosed envelope

NOTICE: Wisconsin customers take notice of taxable items listed on Order Blank, Page 17.

THE KIND OF SAP BAG
YOU CAN THROW AWAY AFTER EACH SEASON

Patented in U.S. and Canada

THE SAP-SAK

SOME OF ITS FEATURES —

SPACE SAVING — See illustration.

LOW COST —
Complete unit costs much less than any other good collecting system.

LIGHT WEIGHT —
No heavy carrying. Unit weighs less than a pound. (Metal bucket and cover weighs 4 lbs.) One man can carry up to 40 or 50 Sap Saks with ease.

COVERED —
Every unit positively covered. Cover is integral part of unit. No extra handling of covers.

TRANSPARENT —
Contents can be seen from a distance — saving unnecessary trips to trees already gathered. Allows ultraviolet rays to penetrate sap and insures sterile sap. Allows detection of any unusual condition of sap.

FLEXIBLE —
Not damaged by freezing or other weather conditions.

SIZE —
Holds 16 quarts. Equal to most buckets.

SUSPENSION —
Hangs directly on spout — most any conventional type spout without a hook.

EMPTYING —
Pivots to right or left directly on spout without removing from tree. Cover directs sap into gathering pail.

HANDLE —
Has sturdy handle for convenient carrying.

TREE ATTACHMENT —
Does not blow off tree in high winds or storm.

QUICK ASSEMBLY —
About 30 seconds.

NO WASHING —
Disassemble and discard the bag. Use new clean bag next season. (Note: Bag can be washed and reused if desired.)

AND NOW — The "TO-GETHER PUTTER" for quick assembling. Floor Model — **$35.00** One included free with purchase of 1000 Sap-Sak Units.

Well — not really new anymore. Hundreds of thousands are used each year.

SAP SAK HOLDERS ONLY
Packed 25 to ctn.
Weight 25 lbs.

Less than 100 units $1.25 ea.
100 Units or more   1.15 ea.

SAP SAKS FOR ABOVE
SINGLE SEAL
Less than 100 .... .13 ea.
100 .... .12 ea.
1000 .... .11 ea.

DOUBLE SEAL
Less than 100 .... .18 ea.
100 .... .17 ea.
1000 .... .15 ea.

Sap Saks wt. 12 lbs. per 100

Spouts for above .... .30 ea.

See page 6 for other kinds

TRIAL KIT

10 COMPLETE UNITS

Complete with Cast Spouts

**$20.00
Prepaid**

25 COMPLETE UNITS

Complete with Cast Spouts

$45.00 Postpaid

**SAMPLE UNIT
COMPLETE**
(Including Spout)

Postpaid **$1.95**

NOTE THE SPACE SAVING

100 Sap-Saks
Weighs less than 100 lbs.
and total cost ($122.00)

Box SAP SAK

24" x 24" x 18"

NOW SEE THE DIFFERENCE —
— WITH BUCKETS AND COVERS

Total Cost ($370.00)

100 Metal Buckets   100 Covers

Weighs about 400 lbs.

The complete Sap-Sak unit consists of a rigid HOLDER which is also a COVER with a band that supports a special made throw-away bag.

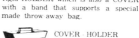

COVER - HOLDER

BAND

BAG

Quickly assembled (about 30 seconds). Open end of bag is slipped thru band - folded over band and set into cover.

Pivots to right or left for emptying. No need to remove from spout.

OR — can be carried anywhere — has sturdy handles.

EQUIPMENT AND SUPPLIES   **23**

LIGHT-WEIGHT

TREE TAPPING MACHINES

AND NOW... YOU CAN USE YOUR CHAIN SAW TO TAP YOUR TREES

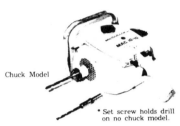

Chuck Model

* Set screw holds drill on no chuck model.

We can supply drilling attachment for most chain saws — but please notice. the attachment fits on your engine on the opposite side from the starter and .f your starter is on the right side then you use a regular right hand bit or drill, but if starter is on the left then you use a left hand drill.

Ordering Instruction
Give make and model of chain saw.

Left Hand Drills are listed on page 6. Just note which side your starter is on so you know which drill to order. Most saws use L.H. Only McCulloch and Poulan have some models using right hand bits.

PLEASE NOTE —

Drillgine and Piston Drill Tappers have not proven very satisfactory, so not shown here.

However, we will supply them on request.

We Carry The Following Drill Attachments In Stock To Fit Your Chain Saw

Part No.		
60	Fits McCulloch Early 10 Series, No chuck (Use R.H. bit)	$22.00
	also fits Poulan 201 - 202 - 203 - 221 - 222 - 245 - 252	
61A	Fits McCulloch Early 10 Series, W/chuck (Use R.H. bit)	32.00
	also fits Poulan 201 - 202 - 203 - 221 - 222 - 245 - 252	
62	Fits McCulloch PM-6 & Mini-Mac 6, No chuck (Use L.H. bit)	20.00
	Warning — This model saw has only 3/8" crank shaft and easily broken, so we recommend next size saw.	
64	Fits Homelite XL - XL 12 - Super XL, No chuck (Use L.H. bit)	22.00
	also fits Poulan 400 - 361 and Pioneer 1100	
64A	Fits Homelite XL - XL 12 - Super XL, W/chuck (Use L.H. bit	32.00
65	Fits Remington 754, No chuck, (Use L.H. bit)	23.00
66	Fits Homelite 101-102-103-104, No chuck (Use L.H. bit)	23.00
67	Fits McCulloch 250 - Mac 15, No chuck (Use L.H. bit)	23.00
68	Fits Homelite XL 700 - XL 800, No chuck (Use L.H. bit)	23.00
69	Fits Remington PL 4 - PL 5, No chuck (Use L.H. bit)	23.00
70	Fits Pioneer Holiday II, 970 - 1022 - 2071, No chuck (Use L.H. bit)	23.00
71	Fits Homelite EZ Automatic 1970, No chuck (Use L.H. bit)	23.00
72	Fits Homelite EZ 1970, No chuck (Use L.H. bit)	23.00
73	Fits Homelite C-51, C-52, No chuck (Use L.H. bit)	23.00
74	Fits Homelite C-5, No chuck (Use L.H. bit)	23.00
75	Fits McCulloch D-44, No chuck (Use R.H. bit)	23.00
77A	Fits McCulloch D-44, W/chuck (Use R.H. bit)	32.00
78	Fits Wright C-40, No chuck (Use L.H. bit)	23.00
79	Fits Homelite XL-500, No chuck (Use L.H. bit)	23.00
80	Fits Homelite 250 EZ Automatic, No chuck (Use L.H. bit)	23.00
81	Fits Homelite XL-400, No chuck (Use L.H. bit)	23.00
82	Fits Skill 1610 - Lombard Pony, No chuck (Use L.H. bit)	23.00
83	Fits Pioneer 1073, 1074, 970, 2071, 2073, P-20, P-25, P-21, P-26, P-28, No chuck (Use L.H. bit)	23.00
84	Fits McCulloch (New) 10-10 Pro 60 & 80 (Model with L.H. thread), No chuck (Use L.H. bit)	32.00
84A	Fits McCulloch (New) 10-10 Pro 60 & 80 (Model with R.H. thread), No chuck (Use L.H. bit)	32.00
85	Fits Stihl 040-AV, No chuck (Use L.H. bit)	23.00
86	Fits Homelite 150-Automatic, No chuck (Use L.H. bit)	23.00
87	Fits John Deere - Remington 8 - 34CC - and Mighty-Mac, No chuck (Use L.H. bit)	23.00
88	Fits Poulan XXV - Jonsered Little Jon - Huskie Jr. - Allis Chal. 125 - Dayton 14 - L.W. Wright 25 - Sears L.W., No chuck (Use L.H. bit)	23.00
89	Fits Poulan Model 223, No chuck (Use L.H. bit)	23.00
90	Fits Jonsered Model 50 & 51, No chuck (Use L.H. bit)	23.00
91	Fits Stihl Model 015 & 020 AV, No chuck (Use L.H. bit)	23.00
	(Following attachments fit over clutch drum)	
85A-S2	Fits Stihl 040 - 031 - 030, No chuck (Use L.H. spade bit)	32.00
85B-S1	Fits Stihl 020 - 021, No chuck (Use L.H. spade bit)	32.00
P1	Fits Pioneer small, No chuck (Use L.H. spade bit)	32.00
P2	Fits Pioneer Medium, No chuck (Use L.H. spade bit)	32.00
M1	Fits McCulloch Mac 6, No chuck (Use L.H. spade bit)	32.00
M2	Fits McCulloch New 10 Series, No chuck (Use L.H. spade bit)	32.00
JP	Fits Small Jonsered or Poulan, No chuck (Use L.H. spade bit)	32.00
P1	Fits Partner, No chuck (Use L.H. spade bit)	32.00
H1	Fits Homelite EZ 150 - 101, No chuck (Use L.H. spade bit)	32.00
H2	Fits Homelite 102 - 103 - 104 - 113 - 114 - 123 - 350, No chuck, (Use L.H. spade bit)	32.00
PL	Fits Poulan Little Jon, No chuck (Use L.H. spade bit)	32.00
F	Fits Frontier, No chuck (Use L.H. spade bit)	32.00
R	Fits Sears, Roper, No chuck (Use L.H. spade bit)	32.00

— All Attachments Postpaid —

Check with us for other models as we may have them available.
Please Note: — "No chuck" type (see picture*) has sleeve holder with allen screws to hold bit and sleeve takes 3/8" shank bit only. All left hand drills (7/16") that we sell, have the 3/8" shank. You will note that the McCulloch 10 series use right hand bits. All "chuck"models have regular adjustable chucks with key.

Now for 1978 ~~~~~~~~~~

Phone: 715 - 449-2057
715 - 449-2536

We have a complete evaporator line so you can choose any make you want.

VERMONT - GRIMM - SMALL BROTHERS
LIGHTNING - LEADER - KING

But order early
for assured delivery

IF YOU NEED NEW PANS OR OTHER PARTS — DON'T WAIT UNTIL SEASON IS HERE — ORDER NOW!

WE SPECIALIZE IN OIL FIRE INSTALLATIONS!

We can convert your own evaporator to oil fire, or we have a do-it-yourself kit, whereby you can install your own.

We furnish everything and with complete instructions.

You can save time — worry — dirt — labor and make Maple Syrup for $1.25 per gallon or less for cost of fuel. Figure on using about 3 gallons of fuel oil to produce 1 gal. of syrup.

Just flip a switch to start or stop. Oil burning together with our automatic syrup draw-off, gives you attention free operation. Can you afford to burn wood?

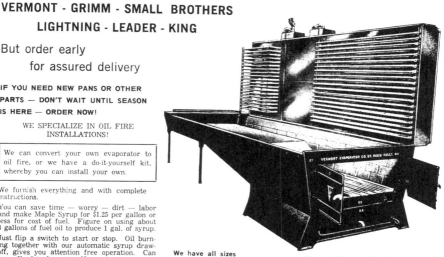

We have all sizes in stock
2 x 4 — 2 x 6
2 x 8 — 3 x 8
3 x 10 — 3 x 12
4 x 12 — 4 x 14
4 x 16 — 5 x 16
6 x 20

Write for information and prices on a size to fit your operation.

View of Vermont Special Evaporator showing Bottom Construction of Pans

As this catalog is being printed, we have these used Evaporators ready to go all shop checked and complete.

1 — 2 x 6 Grimm (New pans)
1 — 2 x 8 Vermont
1 — 3 x 8 Vermont (New pans)
1 — 3 x 10 Leader
1 — 5 x 16 King
1 — 5 x 16 Vermont
1 — 4 x 16 Vermont
1 — 4 x 12 Vermont (New pans)
We have all sizes of new units.

DO YOU HAVE NATURAL GAS OR LOW COST PROPANE?

If so — we have gas burners for your evaporator. No electricity needed.
Clean — Efficient

Wanted to Buy — Used Evaporators or Old Evaporator Arches.
Can use just the castings if rest is bad.

WE CAN SUPPLY MOST EVAPORATOR SIZES WITH REBUILT ARCHES — THUS SAVING YOU $500.00 OR MORE.

Modernize with an ANIWA STEAM HOOD for your evaporator

All aluminum — shipped to you complete, all assembled. Tell us length and width and make of evaporator, and distance from top of pans to roof. Eliminates all steam in room and doesn't spoil roof by making a large opening. This new idea is really working and becoming more popular each year. Requires no electricity — no fan.

These come complete with telescoping vent pipe. This allows raising hood for cleaning or removing pans. Vent pipe canopy also included. Small sizes have two inspection doors on each side. Larger sizes have three. Built-in channels carry off any condensation to end or corner drains

Pick up here if you can. Easily hauled on a pickup or trailer. If we ship — add $40.00 for crating.

3 ft. evaporator	**$395.00**	5 ft. evaporator	**$575.00**
4 ft. evaporator	**495.00**	6 ft. evaporator	**650.00**

SEE THE NEW SYRUP CAN ON PAGE 14

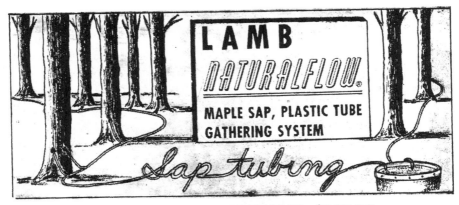

LAMB ELECTRIC TREE TAPPER $235.00

1978 Parts and Price List

Subject To Any Factory Changes — Most Active Items in Stock

Part No.	Description	Price
33-U	Branch Line Poly-Vinyl ultra violet sap tubing 5/16" I. D. furnished in 500' coils	$ 6.00 per 100'
34	Nylon Tees 5/16"	12.00 per 100
35-X	5/16" Special 4 ribbed quick thaw tubing in 500' coils for very cold bushes (only)	9.00 per 100'
36	Nylon spiles 5/16" for 7/16" tapping bit Old style (obsolete).	12.00 per 100
37	Tool for inserting and removing No. 36 spiles	4.00 each
38-F	Auger bit file	˙1.00 each
39	Adapter from 5/16" Lamb sap tubing to 1/4" iron pipe male thread	.35 each
43-U	1/2" Main line ultra violet pipe (water pipe size) furnished in 100' and 400' coils	12.00 per 100'
44-U	3/4" Main line ultra violet pipe (water pipe size) furnished in 100' and 300' coils	16.00 per 100'
45-U	1" Main line ultra violet pipe (water pipe size) furnished in 100' and 200' coils	25.00 per 100'
46	Connector to hook 5/16" tubing together	12.00 per 100'
48	1/2" Main line tee to take 4 Lamb 5/16" tubing line	1.00 each
49	3/4" Main line tee to take 4 Lamb 5/16" tubing	1.00 each
49A	1" tee to take 4-5/16" tubing lines	1.50 each
50	Tool for pulling tubing off fitting	15.00 each
51	All stainless steel clamps for above tee 1/2", 3/4" and 1"	.60 each
52	1/2" Quick clamps	.05 each
53	3/4" Quick clamps	.05 each
54	1" Quick clamps	.10 each
55	Pliers to install quick clamps	5.00 each

PUMPS FOR WASHING TUBING

58	1/4" Bronze gear pump (only)	45.00

PUMPS FOR GATHERING SAP

62	3/4" bronze gear pump 20 g.p.m. at 1700 r.p.m.	85.00
63	1" bronze gear pump 28 g.p.m. at 1700 r.p.m.	110.00
66	Caps for tee 5/16"	3.00 per 100
66A	Cap for 1/2"	.25 each
66B	Cap for 3/4"	.35 each
66C	Cap for 1"	.50 each

WIRE TIES TO HOLD MAIN LINE TUBING TO AERIAL WRES

67	Spout plug for ≠78-S Spout	6.00 per 100
68	1/2" pipe size 4" long 1000 per coil	4.00 per 1000
69	3/4" pipe size 5" long (1000 per coil)	4.00 per 1000
70	1" pipe size 6" long (500 per coil)	4.00 per 1000
71	Hand tying tool for above	1.50 each
77	No. 13 Aluminum Fence wire 2-1/2"	1.00 per 100
78	Combination 5/16" Vented Spile for 7/16" tapping bit	25.00 per 100
78S	5/16" spile (No vent) for 7/16" tapping bit	20.00 per 100
83	Tool for removing No. 78 spile	5.50
84	Sap collector 1/2" or 3/4"	1.50
88	Lamb electric tree tapping drill complete with Pack Rack - 12 volt battery. Cord from battery to drill cord. Electric Drill Holster and belt. Battery box and 1 No. 38 tapping bit.	210.00
89	Lamb 12 volt electric tree tapping drill only	120.00
90	25 ft. cord to attach 12 volt drill to any 12 volt battery with battery snap-on clips	15.00

COUPLINGS

101	Plastic couplings 1"	.60 each
102	Plastic couplings 3/4"	.55 each
103	Plastic couplings 1/2"	.50 each
104	Plastic reducing couplings 1" x 3/4"	.85 each
105	Plastic reducing couplings 1" x 1/2"	.70 each
106	Plastic reducing couplings 3/4" x 1/2"	.50 each

PLASTIC ADAPTER, TO CONNECT PLASTIC TUBING TO PIPE THREAD

107	1"	.55 each
108	3/4"	.50 each
109	1/2"	.45 each
110	Plastic tees 1"	.90 each
111	Plastic tees 3/4"	.75 each
112	Plastic tees 1/2"	.70 each
113	Plastic Reducing tees 1" x 1" x 3/4"	1.15 each
114	Plastic Reducing tees 1" x 1" x 1/2"	1.15 each
115	Plastic Reducing tees 3/4" x 3/4" x 1/2"	.90 each

20 SPILE GET ACQUAINTED KIT

500 ft. 5/16" No. 33-U Sap Tubing
20 No. 78 - 5/16" Spiles
20 No. 34 - 5/16" Tees
3 No. 66 Caps
2 No. 46 - 5/16" Connector

$45.00
POSTPAID

Specifications and prices subject to change without notice

SEE PAGE 10 FOR NEW SAP VACUUM PUMP SYSTEM!

SAPFLO PELLETS

SAPFLO TAP HOLE PELLETS
(Made by the Vicksburg Chemical Co.)

Producers that have tried all makes of pellets tell us that the Sap-Flo — last longer — are more uniform in size and shape — and give the best all around results.

No. 2   No. 1   No. 3   No. 4

You Can't Afford to Not Use Tap Hole Pellets

No. 1 Some seasons they will double your sap flow. At their low cost, they are very cheap insurance.

500 Pack $6.00 — Add .85 Postage
250 Pack $3.25 — Add .85 Postage

No. 2   ## FERMABAN

Prevents Syrup From Spoiling

Fully approved. One jar treats 128 gallons of syrup. Costs about 6c per gallon of syrup.   Price **$6.00**
Stickers advising this additive used, Roll of 500 **$2.00**

MYVEROL   No. 3

Along with pure maple syrup this product makes home confection cooking fun. For profitable sales use MYVEROL for your commercial confections. It keeps the good moisture in and the bad out. The results will please you and your pocketbook.

2 oz. $ .65
Price: 1 lb. can **$3.50** — 4 oz. **$1.00**
Add .85 Postage

MAPLE "QUICK" SAP DEFOAMER — Purest-most-effective.

No. 4 Puts foam down instantly, and holds for a long time. Another Vicksburg time saver.
Now packed in plastic dispensing bottle.   8 oz. Bottle   Price **$1.75**
Add .85 Postage

SAP METERS
Approved Sanitary Type

Install in sap line anywhere. Registers every gallon going through. Operates with or without pressure. A necessity when buying sap. No measuring or guess work. We recommend you order with reset dial — quickly reset reading back to zero.

¾" with fittings (cap. up to 30 gal. per min.) with reset dial 275.00
1" with fittings (cap. up to 50 gal. per min.) with resent dial $325.00
1½" with fittings (cap. up to 120 gal. per min.) with reset dial $425.00

The Maple Syrup Manual is back in print at this date.

Price $3.50

SEE THE NEW
SYRUP CANS
on Page 14

AUTOMATIC SYRUP DRAW-OFF

6 VOLT AUTOMATIC SYRUP DRAW-OFF
(Picture at right)
¾" — **$200.00**   1" size — **$225.00**
Includes fittings.
State name of evaporator.
No more messy, sticky sampling — testing — watching.
Just set the control at whatever thickness you want to draw-off syrup and The Automatic does the rest. As fast as syrup reaches the thickness you set it at, it automatically runs out into your container. Shuts off immediately as syrup becomes thinner. Automatic self-adjusts to barometric pressure changes.
Does not interfere with present manual draw-off.
(All features shown here apply also to unit on right).
Thermo Control only **$100.00**

— New in 1974 —
LIQUID LEVEL CONTROL
for evaporator pans.
$150.00
A real safety feature
(Not pictured)

We recommend this unit —
110 VOLT AUTOMATIC SYRUP DRAW-OFF
This unit also available in 6 volt.
(Not pictured)
**NEW IN 1960 - Hundreds in use today
Now with new control**
½" — Unit only — 110 volt — **$200.00**
Unit complete with two sets all brass fittings including brass gate valves — plugs, ells, nipples, bushings, unions, (so you can change from side to side of syrup pan.) Electric outlet box with cord and plug-in. Complete with instructions.
For 2' & 3' evap. ½" unit **$250.00**
For 4' & 5' evap. ¾" unit **$350.00**
*For 6' evap. 1" unit **$425.00**
* (Recommended for 6 ft. evaporators)

SAP SPOUTS -

STEEL TIN PLATED
GRIMM SAP SPOUTS

GRIMM 7/16" with hooks.

Per 100 $34.00

Add 90c for postage

Can be used with new Sap-Sak by removing hook
and bending lip downward.
Vermont not available due to factory problems. But we can
supply the Grimm Spout which is similar.

New style made of
aluminum 7/16" only

Per 100 $25.00

Add 85c for Postage.

Can be used with Sap Sak
by cutting notch in top.

**THE BIG
SELLER**

Light to handle — Low cost
Will not rust — Last a lifetime
if not abused.

Extra hooks **$6.00** per 100
Fits Grimm or Vermont spouts

SPOUT DRIVER	
spouts **$2.00**	
For Vermont or Grimm	

WARNER 7/16" cast
aluminum with hook.

$35.00 per 100

Add $1.00 postage if mailed.

Not suitable for Sap-Saks.

Add 3¢ each for lots less than 100 for all spouts.

More In Demand Each Year
ALUMINUM SAP SPOUT

Made in Canada

Approved by
The Department of Agriculture
of the Province of Quebec

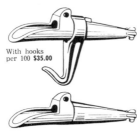

With hooks
per 100 **$35.00**

Without hooks **$30.00** per 100

Add 95c Postage

Extra hooks 6c each.

We recommend this spout (hookless) for the new Sap-Saks.

Manufacturer claims
with this spout, you
will obtain these out-
standing advantages:
1. Strong and sturdy
light metal rust proof.
2. It is perfectly cir-
cular to fit closely in
the hole.
3. It has four rest
points which assure
the solidity.
4. It allows you to
obtain 25% MORE
SAP than with the
old type spouts - - -
(sufficient to cover
their cost in one
season!)
5. It gives you a first
quality product (low-
est bacteria count).
6. It does not oxyde
the wood; the wound
is therefore healing
rapidly.

Sample .50 Postpaid

SOULE STYLE SPOUTS now
made of alloy for plastic bags
or new Sap-Saks.
$30.00 per 100. Postage $1.00

GENUINE SOULE — Mallable, Hookless   **Per 100 $70.00**

Add 3c each for lots less than 100 for all spouts.

A Spout Made of
Nylon

Pure White   Very Sanitary

Practically unbreakable, light
to handle, gentle on tap hole.
Will not bruise the wood.

Users are well pleased.

Will not rust.

$26.00 per 100

Add 85c Postage

We at Reynolds Sugar Bush want to thank you
for your business through the years. Being
actual syrup makers ourselves, we try to test
most all types of equipment under actual syrup
making conditions before we sell it to others.
As our business has continued to grow through
your loyal patronage, we are able to carry a
better and more complete line of syrup making
supplies. We are bringing you a better selec-
tion by giving you a choice of equipment from
many different manufacturers.

If you have suggestions for improving our service, please feel free to tell us. Also tell us
if there are other items that we should be carrying for your needs.

Again we thank you.

TAPPING BITS
Sugar Tree Style
Screw Point short type now made for brace or power

Irwin Pattern 3/8" - 7/16" - 1/2" **$4.25**
These come with square shank as pictured.
Cut off for power tapper.
We find this out-drills & outlasts the higher priced drills
when used with right hand chain saw attachment.

Left Hand Drill 7/16" for use with most
chain saws (3/8" shank) .... Ea. **$6.50**
Left Hand Flat Spade type Bit 7/16"
¼" shank .... Ea. **$2.00**

CLEVELAND — Maple Tree Drills with spur point.
STYLE

For Brace — 7/16" .... Square shank **$9.00**
For Tapper — 7/16" .... Round shank **$9.00**
Bit File **$2.00**
Use Tap Hole ellets — No need to ream.

READ YOUR MAPLE DIGEST

It used to be free to all Syrup Makers but not anymore.
If you are not on mailing list, send us your name and
a buck and we will try to getyou on it. Better yet —
join Your State association and you will automatically
get the Digest.

SAP GATHERING PAILS
BUCKETS AND BAGS

— See Front Cover For New Sap-Sak —

THE VERMONT COVER

V type shown on bucket below This is a better made cover. — Double rolled edge. — Fits most all Roof Type Buckets.

75¢ Each

The Finest Heavy Duty
SAP BUCKETS
15 - Quart Galvanized

Each $3.25

A NEW TYPE GATHERING PAIL OF POLYETHLENE
20 Quart Size

Unbreakable
Sanitary
Will never
rust.

$8.50 Each

FLAT COVERS
85¢ Each

Extra wires **$6.00 per 100**
The Grimm Flat Cover shown on bucket below, will cover most all types buckets, including the tin cherry cans which have no top rim. This cover hinges directly on spout. Entirely independent of bucket.

Another New Very Sanitary
BUCKET OF
Polyethlene
18 Qt. Size

$1.60

SEAMLESS ALUMINUM GATHERING PAIL

Light to carry, yet has 24 Quart capacity.
Heighth from bottom of the pail to the handle: 16½". Lowered handle permitting to walk in the brush at arm's length without touching snow. Bottom allowing easy lifting of the pail. One piece — no seams. A sellout every year.

$19.00 Each

VERMONT GALVANIZED
THE MOST POPULAR GATHERING PAIL
18 QUART
$15.00

POWER BUCKET WASHER

Let a Motor do this work for you. Washing buckets is a disagreeable job by hand. This machine is designed especially for this job.
Complete with motor (Special Brush) **$195.00**
Complete less motor (includes pulley & belt) **$180.00**
(¼ or ½ horse electric motor required), or use Tapper motor.

Bucket Washing Brush only **$20.00**
(full bucket size) Tapered to fit all size buckets. Will last for thousands of bucket washings. Build your own Washer — Just attach to a shaft and drive with any motor or mount this brush in place of agitator in old washing machine.

NEED A NEW SMOKE STACK?
ALL SIZES IN STOCK — BASES & ROUND

Just tell us your size diameter. Measure arch collar casting when ordering base.

We have a few used small Steam Boilers in stock.

Old Style
SOULE
PLASTIC SAP BAGS
Per 100 **$175.00**

A NEW ITEM — IN 1964
We have sold thousands since
A Special Made POLYETHLENE LINER
for Sap Buckets

Slip inside any bucket. Makes any rusty or leaky pail usable again. Makes a very sanitary container and is sap or waterproof. Can be washed and used from year to year or just thrown away. They are inexpensive enough for this. Eliminates washing buckets.

$8.00 per 100

Special Purchase of several thousand USED sap buckets. Seamless aluminum and in good condition. Requires spout with hook.
10 Qt. size selling at $1.25

SAP AND SYRUP
TESTING INSTRUMENTS

Hydrometer, for hot or cold syrup, ea. ....$ 6.00
Hydrometer, for testing cold sap. ea. 6.00
Extra long Hydrometer
range 1° - 10° Brix Scale for sap 7.00
Plated tin testing cup, each 5.00
    Stainless Steel 6.00
This is a better cup — has platform bottom and
hooks on side of pan (cup shown below).

Long style Brix, Range 59 to 71 Hydrometer
for syrup, each ....$ 8.00
Same in Range 49 to 61, each 8.00
Plated Tin Cup for long style Hydrometers.... 5.50
    Stainless Steel for same 7.00

Thermometer needed for making sugar ....$ 9.95
Thermometer (same) made by Taylor 21.00
Thermometer, adjustable scale 20.00

AYRES HYDROTHERM

Test syrup at any temperature, each $19.50
Testing cup for above, ea. $4.50 — Stainless $6.00
Add 85c Postage to any item above.

The newest and most accurate syrup testing. Installs on side of pan. Requires no adjusting. Always correct. Approved by Research Lab. Actual temp. range 205° to 225° - (picture incorrect.

Price with two fittings
(one for each side of pan)

Large size made by Taylor

**Stainless Steel
Testing Cup
$6.00**

$75.00

DIAL
THERMOMETER

6" scale. Bi-metal element stainless
steel, fits any evaporator.
    6" stem $33.00
    Smaller size, dial $23.00
Brass fittings, pair .... $ 8.00
(Needed to install in pan)

And Now — The Refractomer

For extreme accuracy in testing for
sugar solids, the kind used in laboratories. Needs only one drop for testing.
Brix Range for syrup 45° to 82° **$165.00**
Brix Range for sap 0° to 32° **$165.00**
Brix Range 0° to 82° **$195.00**
Comes complete with leather case
and carrying straps.

EVAPORATOR NEED REPAIRS?

Bring it to our new service shop, where we can
usually repair any make of evaporator.

Every Syrup Maker Needs This

**MORE POPULAR EVERY YEAR
THIS IS THE ORIGINAL**

BOTTLE GAS BURNER — SYRUP
FINISHING SYSTEM

Everybody has copied this but they can't match our
price. A necessity with any make evaporator. Gives it
greater capacity.   This is the IDEAL outfit for the
modern syrup maker.

POSITIVE HEAT CONTROL.   Cheap operation.   Less
than 5c per gallon of syrup. Triple tubular burners with
individual controls.   Each of these has an output of
30,000 B.T.U.'s — total 90,000 B.T.U.'s. Stands 36" high.
Pan is English Tin Plate, with outlet box and draw-off
gate. Pan measures approximately 2' x 4' x 11". Nearly
all the larger syrup makers have this outfit. Makes it
much easier to bring your syrup to exact weight.

Complete $365.00
Burner only 200.00
Pan only 165.00
With Stainless Steel Pan add 135.00
Another model with jet style burners and complete
with heavy duty stainless steel pan with divider
and rugged stand 550.00
Aluminum Steam Hood. sliding doors. complete
with aluminum vent pipe. to fit either above units 135.00
With 6" Dial Thermometer installed add 40.00
With Mercury Thermometer installed add 70.00

See the New SYRUP CANS on Page 14

Old Style But —
BRAND NEW
SAP PANS

Choice of three metals —

	Galv.	English Tin	Stainless Steel
23 x 17 x 11	$ 55.00	$ 80.00	$ 95.00
47 x 28 x 11	95.00	145.00	265.00
47 x 28 x 8	90.00		290.00
72 x 28 x 8	110.00		395.00

with outlet and faucet add $20.00

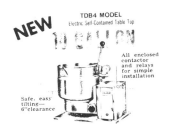

NEW

TDB4 MODEL
Electric Self-Contained Table Top

All enclosed
contactor
and relays
for simple
installation

Safe, easy
tilting—
6"clearance

And Now A STEAM KETTLE

For anyone even without a steam boiler. All electric, all stainless steel. You don't even need a water connection. Ideal for candy making or syrup finishing. You do need electricity. Water is self contained and seldom needs attention. Cook within minutes and without danger of burning. We have made tons of maple candy with these.

5 Gallon $1,325.00   10 Gallon $1,750.00

Subject to factory price change.

Vermont Syrup Filter Tanks

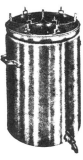

English Tin 35 Gal.
with Steel Stand
Detachable Faucet
$195.00
Same as above only all stainless
steel with chrome non-drip faucet
36" x 36" size — **$245.00**

English Tin, 30 Gal.
Tray with 3 Filter Bags
or Screen Tray with
Orlon Flat Filter.
(State Choice)
Detachable Faucet
Complete with Cover
$150.00

Want Sparkling Clear Syrup?
A PRESSURE FILTER IS THE ANSWER

Many styles and capacities and of course price, depending on your needs.

A size with capacity of 100 gallons per hour — depending on amount of sediment, uses square filter papers and filter aid. If syrup is allowed to settle, capacity of filter is increased. Complete with motor, pump, season supply of papers and 15 lbs of filter aid **$795.00**

Filter press comes crated and is shipped either motor freight or rail express.

See larger Pressure Filters on next page.

Filter Aid — 50 lb. bag **$11.00**
Extra Papers for above (400) **$11.00**

Filter Bag Liner
**INCREASES LIFE OF BAGS
SAVES TIME**

ORLON
BAG

75c ea. — 3 for $2.00 — Doz. $7.00
Add 10c each for postage.
No need to remove filter bag from syrup filtering tank. Just remove liner from bag, rinse out solids in hot or cold water and replace. Liner has long life with careful use.

ORLON FLAT FILTERS

24" x 24"	$7.50
24" x 30"	8.50
24" x 36"	9.50
30" x 36"	13.00
36" x 36"	14.00

**WOOL OR ORLON
FILTER BAGS**

Regular size, pure wool, ea. **$8.50**
Extra large size, pure wool, ea. 10.00
Orlon Filter Bag, large size 10.00
  (Orlon has many advantages over wool)
Flannel Inner Bag to use with above
(saves washing so often, hangs inside)
Use over and over .... 3 for $4.50
Rayon Prefilter paper 36" x 36", ea. 75c
Doz. 7.00

100 Yard Roll 40.00

ARE YOU READY??

FAST CAN OR BOTTLE FILLING

THE SIPHON FILLER

A simple and economical machine for bottling or canning your syrup. Needs no electricity. Easy to operate. Fills as fast as you can handle containers. Filling stops at any depth you set machine. Handles most any size container. All stainless contact parts. Use as many filling tubes as you wish.

Machine complete with 5 filling tubes **$895.00**
The Popular One — Smaller size with
2 filling tubes, complete all stainless top **395.00**
Extra Saddles (for mounting tubes) each **7.50**
Electric Heating Element installed add $33.00
Extra stainless steel filling tubes, each **53.00**

---

1 used rotary style siphon filler with 18 filler tubes - Motor driven, complete **$600.00**

PRESSURE FILTERS

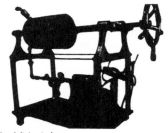

One left in stock —
Used 14" square plate Pressure Filter, floor model
Complete and like new (stainless) **$5000.00**

For low cost moderate size Filter - new, see page 9

IT'S FINALLY HERE!
The NEW
SAP-SUCKER VACUUM
SYSTEM

Forget Complicated Dump Units — Vacuum Tanks — Floats — Switches — Tricky Controls, etc.

Start with one pump and add more as you need them or as your system grows. One unit will handle up to 400 taps. REVERSABLE — DOES NOT OVERHEAT — DON'T DISCOLOR SAP — FREEZE PROOF — CAN RUN DRY.

ELECTRIC — GASOLINE — BOTTLE GAS

Automatic start and stop switch available on electric model.

One pump with bracket and pulley **$160.00**
One pump , electric, complete **355.00**
One pump, gasoline, complete **395.00**
One pump, bottle gas, complete **475.00**
Each add-on pump **140.00**

SHOWING 3 PUMP UNITS BELOW —

NO ELECTRICITY IN YOR BUSH?
(Optional kill switch illustrated on gasoline model shown.)

SMOKE STACK COVER

Easy to attach and it really works.

To fit 10"	16" Stacks	$35.00
To fit 17"	24" Stacks	45.00

Be sure and state size of your stack.

HEAVY DUTY GATHERING TANKS

5 bbl. size	$350.00
7½ bbl. size	450.00
9½ bbl. size	525.00

Corrugated Round End Galvanized Tanks

All have 2" outlet.

Made for hauling sap. Heavy guage. All soldered seams.

Splash Boards   Wisconsin made tanks.

3 bbl. size, 2' x 2' x 4'	97 Gal.	**$135.00**
4½ bbl. size, 2' x 2' x 6'	150 Gal.	**150.00**
6 bbl. size, 2' x 2' x 8'	200 Gal.	**170.00**
8 bbl. size, 2½' x 2' x 8'	250 Gal.	**185.00**
9½ bbl. size, 3' x 2' x 8'	300 Gal.	**195.00**
12 bbl. size, 3' x 2' x 10'	390 Gal.	**245.00**
Screen or Strainer for above tanks		**24.00**

All tanks have 2" outlet for fast drawing.
2" flexible hose, wire reinforced, with brass coupling, fits above tanks .... ea. **$35.00**
Sap receiving funnel to fit 3" conductor pipe ea. **35.00**

This is no gimmick — Read your Digest Protect Your Sap and Syrup With —

GERMICIDAL LAMPS AND FIXTURES

COMPLETE UNIT

Heavy Duty — Fixture — Reflector — Bulb
(Reflector not shown in picture but is included)

High Power Factor (36")	**$39.95**
Extra Bulbs	18.95

Still a Few Left . . .

SAP OR SYRUP STORAGE TANKS

We made a special purchase of heavy steel glass lined tanks with dome shaped ends. Can be used vertical or horizontal. Each has manhole with swing-in door and gasket. Threaded inlet and outlet openings on ends. Two sizes — 2600 gallon and 3600 gallon. Only few left.

7' - 8' in diameter and 8' - 9' high. Also square open top tanks about 8' high and 7½' across. These are heavy steel with glass lining and fully approved for foods. These tanks are used but in perfect condition and ¼ price of new. 15c per gal. Germicidal lamps installed if wanted.

1 — 1500 gallon stainless steel horizontal tank — with man-hole — ladder platform — observation window — a real beauty at only **$995.00**

STAINLESS STEEL TANKS

1 left — Stainless steel 300 gallon horizontal (brand new) tanks at **$500.00** each.

SANITARY PUMPS

— We sell hundreds of these —

Sanitary Pump for Sap or Hot Syrup	**$15.00**
Larger size. Extra shaft bearing, has stainless steel shaft and special impeller for maple sap or hot syrup	22.00
Base for mounting motor and pump	6.50
Self prime pump ¾" rubber impeller	50.00
Extra ¾" impeller	5.50
Flexible coupling for attaching to motor. (State size motor shaft)	3.50

We have larger sizes too for tractor mount.

Self prime pump 1¼" rubber impeller	120.00
Extra 1¼" impeller	12.00
Adapter for tractor drive (state make) for above 1¼" size pump	20.00

Bronze gear pump for pressure filters or other uses. ½" **$50.00**, ¾" **$65.00**, 1" **$70.00**

PORTABLE PUMPS

Self Priming with foot valve

Gas motor mounted on base with large capacity sanitary pump, complete - ready to use (with carrying handle) **$165.00**
Electric motor and pump unit complete **95.00**
Either unit will pump sap most anywhere and will also pump hot syrup. We pump sap over a mile with this pump.

SELF PRIMING PUMPS

Gas Engine Powered

Rubber impeller pump gives excellent suction.

Inlet and outlet ¾" threaded.

$225.00

COLORFUL LABELS — Now that you have the syrup made and canned or bottled — don't stop there. Finish your package with a nice attractive label. — It pays.

ABOVE LABEL now available in pressure sensitive style. Sticks to any surface. Lower price too. (state size)

Large — Medium — Small

Per 100 — **$4.00**

No. 2. New 3 Color Label "Pressure sensitive"
Sticks to anything

3-7/8" x 2-1/2"	Per 100
3-1/8" x 3-1/8"	
3-1/8" x 2-1/8"	**$3.50**

AND — Wrap around labels from "Bob" (beautifully lithographed) to fit pints - quarts - half gallons, as shown on can below. **$6.00 per 100**

No. 3. 4 Color Label
Plain back
Requires label paste
(Shown on Jug - Page 13)

5-5/8" x 3-5/8" - **$3.00** per 100
3-7/8" x 2-1/2" - **$2.50** per 100
2-1/2" x 1-5/8" - **$2.00** per 100

No. 4. Folded Tags for attaching to jugs, pitchers, etc. Punched holes for ribbon or gold chains listed below.
(See picture on page 13)
Space for name, etc. on outside, and space inside for other advertising.
Tags (4 color) per 100 **$3.50**
Gold key chains per 100 **$4.00**

NOTICE — Above Prices Include Printing If Ordered In Lots of 1000 or More

All labels come to you postpaid. Allow 20 days for printing and mailing.

HOW ABOUT NAME STICKERS —
We have gold foil pressure-sensitive stickers printed one color (any name or words) and up to 4 lines as follows: (Order by number and state gold foil stickers and print clearly).

This size up to 3 lines $20.00 for 2,000	No. 1.
This size up to 4 lines $20.00 for 2,000	No. 2.
	No. 3.
This size up to 4 lines $21.00 for 2,000	
	No. 4.
This size up to 4 lines $20.00 for 1,000	

Note:—
The
Price
Change
Here.

NEW PRESSURE SENSITIVE LABELS
Your State Name
(Ideal for Litho Cans on page 14)
Bright Red Printing on Transparent Tape (acetate)
These stickers are ¼" x 1½" and stick to most any surface, and looks like it was printed right on the can or bottle. These labels as well as stickers above work fine on litho cans and plastic jugs.
Roll of 1000 — $11.00 Any name, state or province.

AND FOR WISCONSIN PRODUCERS
THE NEW GRADE A AND FANCY STICKERS
Roll of 1000 — Postpaid **$6.00**
All-state stickers - fancy, Grade A and Grade B
Roll of 1000 - Size 1" — **$6.00**

RUBBER STAMPS
Your Name and Address **$8.50**
Special Ink and Pad - Red, Blue, Green or Black (This is a better stamp & ink) 3.50
Grade Stamps - Fancy - Grade A - Grade B
$2.00 ea. p.p.

Wisconsin only

BICENTENNIAL STICKERS
Red - White and Blue
$10.00 per 1000 Roll

All states

SHIPPING CARTONS
Fits 1 Pint Syrup tins	**$ .20**
Fits 12 Pint Syrup tins	.38
Fits 24 Pint Syrup tins	.47
Fits 1 Quart Syrup tins	.23
Fits 2 Quart Syrup tins	.35
Fits 4 Quart Syrup tins	.35
Fits 12 Quart Syrup tins	.36
Fits One ½ Gallon Syrup tins	.55
Fits Six ½ Gallon Syrup tins	.28
Fits 1 Gallon Syrup tins	.32
Fits 4 Gallon Syrup tins	.65

We also stock a Super Mailing carton for more protection. Pint-Quart, Half Gallon and Gallon. These are double wall with extra end protection Add 50%.
In ordering cartons, be sure and state for what style can
(This is very important)
Gummed Tape for sealing cartons, 3" roll, 600' **$3.50**
Label Paste, holds to tin or glass **$2.00**

CASH IN ON YOUR BOTTLE NECK

EVERYONE WANTS THESE . . . .

SEALING BAND For Your Bottles

This is a cello neck band printed two sides "Pure Maple Syrup". (Red on White). Fits most bottles using 28mm cap. This band gives more "class" to your package as well as a better seal. Also prevents opening by "tasters" and gives more confidence to buying public. Band is slipped loosely over neck of bottle and shrinks tight within minutes. Pack of 500 bands **$6.00**

Also For Larger Sizes

Medium size 38mm fits all pint decanters, refrigerator bottles, gallon & ½ gal. jugs. Pack of 350 **$6.00**
Larger 48mm fits quart decanters and etc. Pack of 300 .... **$6.00**
Add $1.00 Postage
We also stock plain white bands in all 3 sizes.

DECANTER BOTTLES

NOTICE: Above Bands shown in use on bottles below.

½ Gal. Glass Jug 6 per carton at **$3.75** per carton.

Qts. 48mm cap 12 to case, per doz. **$4.25**
Pts. 38mm cap 12 to case, per doz. **3.25**

No. 1 — 28mm cap
No. 2 — 24mm cap
No. 3 — 28mm cap
No. 4 — 28mm cap

No. 5 — 38mm cap

PLAIN ROUND BOTTLES

(Samples of Labels Shown Above)
(Label Prices on Page 12)

1. ¾ Pint Jugs, 12 to ctn., with handle .... per doz. **$3.25**
2. ½ Pint Jugs, 24 to ctn., with handle .... per doz. **3.50**
3. 1 Pint Jugs, 12 to ctn., with handle .... per doz. **4.50**
4. Quart Refrigerator back again in plastic .... per doz. **3.75**
5. 2 oz. sample bottles (not pictured) .... per doz. **2.00**
6. 2/5 Pint, 24 to ctn. .... per doz. **2.95**

HONEY JARS

2 lb. (case 12) **$3.95**
1 lb. (case 24) **$5.75**
½ lb. (case 24) **$5.00**

Qt. 28mm cap 12 to case, doz. **3.95**
Pt. 28mm cap 24 to case, doz. **2.95**
½ Pt. 28mm cap 12-case, doz. **2.85**

NOVELTY MINIATURE BEER BOTTLES

Holds about 2½ oz. Maple Syrup
Pkd. 10 doz to case
$1.80 per doz.
18mm cap

Novelty Miniature WHISKEY FLASKS

Holds about 2½ oz. Maple Syrup
Pkd. 10 doz. to case
18mm cap
$1.80 per doz.

Plain White Caps Included With All Bottles On This Page

Extra Caps Plain White (28mm)............per doz. **.30**
Extra Caps for Half or Gallon Jugs (White Litho)
Also fits pt. decanter and qt. refrigerator bottles (38mm)............ **.48**
Extra Caps, white litho) fits qt. decanter (48mm)............ **.60**

Fancy Litho Red and Gold Maple Syrup Caps (28mm only) .... per doz **.36**

Add 12c per dozen to above glass prices if fancy caps are wanted instead of regular. (28mm only)

We have screw caps to fit any size bottle or tin can. (If in doubt of size, send us an old cap)

NOVELTY CONTAINERS - CERAMIC PACKAGING - Includes Corks — Extra Corks 3c each

2 oz.
6 doz.
per case.
Per doz.
$8.00

OLD STYLE JUG
4 oz.
2 doz. per case
Per doz. **$9.50**
8 oz.
2 doz. per case
Per doz. **$16.00**
16 oz.
2 doz. per case
Per doz. **$21.00**
32 oz.
1 doz. per case
Per doz. **$24.00**

BEAUTIFUL PITCHER
Brown or Green
10 oz.
2 doz. per case
Per doz. **$14.00**

SMALL PITCHER
Brown or Green
3 oz.
2 doz. per case
Per doz. **$9.00**

New Shape PITCHER
Asst. colors
10 oz.
2 doz. per case
$18.00 per doz.

HILLBILLY JUG
complete with Corn Cob Stopper
1 doz. per case
$18.00 per doz.

OLD STYLE JUGS printed in gold lettering - your copy - **Add $1.50 per doz.** — Minimum order 50 doz. Allow 6 weeks.
RED SEALING WAX — Stick .60 ea. Box of 4, $1.75. Bulk Pack $2.00 per lb. For Folded Tags see labels on page (12).

Pack Your Syrup In
Lithographed Cans

Very Colorful — 2 styles - State kind wanted

· No label needed. Inner seals included with most styles.
Space provided for stamping your name and address.

No. 3.   **YELLOW LITHO**
Prices same as covered bridge (at right)
Picture shows "Wisconsin", however we will ship
without any state printed.

PLAIN TIN SYRUP CANS
WITH SCREW CAPS & SEALS
(With proper plating for maple syrup)

5 Gal. have 2½" cap — 1 Gal. & ½ Gal.: 1¾" cap

Quarts, Pints & ½ Pints: 1¼" caps.

	Less than case lot	Case lot	Case Price
Half Pint	ea. .45	300	ea. .43
Pint	ea. .47	252	ea. .45
Quart	ea. .51	147	ea. .50
½ Gallon	ea. .64	50	ea. .62
Gallon	ea. .67	50	ea. .65
5 Gallon Plastic	ea. 3.75		

Something Different —
TINY TIE TAC

MAPLE LEAF DESIGN

Ladies — Get One For Your Husband

Any Syrup Maker Will Treasure This

THIS IS THE FINEST MADE!

STERLING SILVER — $5.00

**THIS IS THE LAST YEAR
FOR THIS STYLE CAN AND
STOCK IS LIMITED.
SEE NEW CAN BELOW.**

No. 4.   **COVERED BRIDGE**

Gallons - ½ Gal. - Qts. have 1¾" opening
Pints and ½ Pints have 1¼" opening

	Less than case lot		Case lot	Case Price
Half Pint	ea. .50		300	ea. .48
Pint	ea. .53		200	ea. .51
Quart	ea. .60		100	ea. .58
Half Gallon	ea. .77		50	ea. .75
One Gallon	ea. .82		50	ea. .80

Note:— We will no longer guarantee Empire cans.

SPECIAL WRENCH FOR CAN OR BOTTLE CAPS

For tightening or loosening
Made of chromed steel — A real dandy
New Style for 28mm only **$3.95**

A BEAUTIFUL
BRAND NEW
LITHOGRAPHED
SYRUP CAN FOR 1978
NOW IN STOCK!

— A REAL QUALITY CAN —

No more rust - Dirty Seams - Leaks

Beautiful Lithographed Maple Scene in Five Colors
Tall Flat Style — Takes less shelf space.
Shaped as plain tins shown at the left.

Gallon Cans have 1¾" opening.
Half Gallon, Quarts and Pints have 1¼" opening.
Half Pints have 1" opening.
All complete with screw caps and seals.

Gallon size	packed 60 per case	.90
Half Gallon size	packed 108 per case	.80
Quart size	packed 147 per case	.55
Pint size	packed 225 per case	.48
Half Pint size	packed 384 per case	.45

THE KRESS STYLE PLASTIC JUG

White with red Printed Maple Scene

5 sizes - ½ Gal, Qts, Pts.
¾ Pt. and ½ Pt.

½ Pt.	48 to ctn.	$23.00	ea. .49
¾ Pt.	24 to ctn.	12.00	ea. .52
Pint	24 to ctn.	12.75	ea. .54
Pint	115 to ctn.	59.75	ea. .53
Quart	12 to ctn.	7.60	ea. .62
Quart	60 to ctn.	36.60	ea. .62
½ Gal.	36 to ctn.	27.00	ea. .77

and now with 38mm cap.

We stock cartons to fit Kress and Bacon Jugs.
Prices same as tin on Page 12.

AND NOW MORE —
PLASTIC JUGS (Bacon)   Bulk Pack — 5 Sizes

Gallon size .... .75	Quart size .... .47
	Pint size .... .42
½ Gal. size .... .65	½ Pint size .... .40

Sugar Sand Solvent

We sell more and more of this each year.

THE WONDERFUL NEW
PAN CLEANING SOLUTION

Store anywhere - it doesn't freeze.
This will positively clean any pan, no matter how badly coated or burned.
Here is something you need, something needed ever since Maple Syrup has been made.
This is a formula solution that really works. Takes off ALL accumulated scale or coating from your syrup pans. Does not harm the metal or your hands.
(It doesn't take out any dents though).

$5.25 per Gallon
$5.00 in lots of 6 gallons or more in 1 gal. plastic jugs.
6 gallons per carton.
Medium size evaporator requires about 2 gallons.
But keep plenty on hand so that you can clean often.
Your better quality syrup will pay you back many times for the use of this cleaner.
We Guarantee Satisfaction.

Shipped Express or Motor Freight collect.

CELLOPHANE BAGS
FOR PACKAGING MAPLE CANDY
(Makes your candy sparkle)
Large size, holds 1 lb. sm. cakes, 200 in box **$7.00**
Med. size, holds ½ lb. sm. cakes, 200 in box **$5.00**
Small size, for individual cakes, 200 in box **$3.00**
Colorful Maple Sugar Labels **$3.00** per 100
Space for name and weight.

REAL NOVEL PACKAGE

Two pc. molded styrofoam with 4-8 oz. glass jars.
Makes excellent gift pack for syrup, honey, etc.
Complete with carton for mailing.   Set each **$1.75**

Packed 24 sets per carton.
Without Glass Jars — Set each **.95**

SYPHONS

FOR OLD STYLE EVAPORATORS

Each $16.95

RUBBER MOLDS For Maple Sugar

Candy Pops Out By Just Flexing The Mold.

Each Piece Is Perfectly Shaped.

Easily Washed In Hot Water

No. 1243 Maple Leaf, 20 Cavities ⅓ oz.	**$ 9.00**
No. 1138 Maple Leaf, 12 Cavities 1 oz.	9.00
No. 1137 Maple Leaf, 8 Cavities 2 oz.	9.00
No. 54 Little Man, 9 Cavities	9.00
No. 1056 Heart, 15 Cavities	9.00
Demonstration, 15 Cavities	7.45
Large Sheet - any size leaf choice	34.00

Many other shapes. Write for circular showing larger sheets and prices.

Few used black rubber molds left at ½ price including Large Fish - Small Fish - Large Indian - 8 oz. Square.

You are invited to the Wisconsin Maple Syrup Festival on May 28, 1978

1978 will be the 28th Annual Wisconsin Maple Syrup Festival and Pancake Day here at Aniwa, Wis. Make plans to attend this year. Date will be May 28, 1978 the last Sunday in May. Thousands of people will be here. There will be top entertainment. Top exhibits and plenty to eat. Plenty of parking. Everybody welcome.

County Agricultural Agents, Extension Foresters, County Home Agents, Dept. of Agriculture, all help with program and administration.

Have you entered the yearly syrup contest? Why not do it this year. Send a quart of your best syrup, so it arrives here not later than May 27th for judging. Entries will be on display and awards announced day of festival. All entries will be given to Wisconsin Maple Council for promotion of Maple Syrup. Even if you don't win an award, you will be contributing to Maple promotion and advertising. Of course anyone wanting their entry returned, may have this done by providing return postage. All winning entries will be shown at the Wisconsin State Fair with the name of producer. WE WILL EXPECT YOU. Bring your family and your friends.

You are now invited to become a member of the International Maple Syrup Intstitute. One of the benefits of being a member — entitles you to use the New Maple Syrup LOGO on or as part of your syrup container label.

This logo on your label identifys your product as being Pure Maple and will be recognized nation wide as a guarantee of quality.

To apply for membership, contact us — or write direct to:

International Maple Syrup Institute
643 Grosvenor Ave.
Montreal, Quebec, H3Y 259

BEGINNERS TRIAL KIT

This includes everything you would need to start a small operation and tap 20 trees.

KIT INCLUDES —

1 — Maple Syrup Manual	**Complete**
20 — Sapflo Taphole Pellets	**$146.00**
20 — Cast Aluminum Sap Spouts	**Delivered**
20 — Sap-Sak Metal Holders	
20 — Double Seal Sap-Saks	**Without Pan**
1 — Syrup Testing Hydrometer	**$64.00**
1 — Testing Cup for Hydrometer	**Delivered**
1 — 7/16" Tapping Bit for Brace	
1 — Wool Syrup Filter	
1 — English Tin Boiling Pan approx. 17 x 23 x 11 in.	

SALT AND PEPPER SHAKERS

This item has no relation to maple syrup, but makes a cute gift item. Filled with granulated maple sugar. We have sold thousands of these.

REAL MINIATURE MILK CANS

Cover lifts out just like regular cans. Sifter part underneath. Very cute.

Set **$1.25** Postpaid

Doz. Sets **$1.00** per set P.P.

Copper or Silver Finish

Made of anodized aluminum.

COLOR STANDARDS

Permanent Colored Glass — Steel Frame, Square Bottles
Extra Sample Bottles

This is the finest.

$98.50

Add $1.00 Postage

 Syrup Grading Sets

Older Style (liquid style)

$5.00

Add 85c Postage

THE 1978 MAPLE STORY — The demand for good table grade syrup is excellent and there is no carryover anywhere. This should give producers new confidence and more incentive, as prices should be at a good level **and the dark syrup market is back.** All grades of syrup are in short supply and all grades will be in good demand. The dark syrup market has fully recovered and prospects are even better. We now have the International Maple Syrup Institute organized, and its highest priority will be to develop new markets and improve existing ones. We hope every producer will support this institute, because it was created by the Maple Industry to help the Maple Industry, and already there is a shortage.

We like to buy in truck tanker loads (4,000 gallons) where we pick up in an area. You keep your drums — so there is none to return. Check with your Local Maple Association for guidance in marketing, and be sure you are a dues paying member. Summary — all time high for prices and demand for 1978 crop.

MAPLE SUGAR AND CANDY EQUIPMENT

Machine For Making Maple Cream
Stainless Steel Parts
Motor Driven
$325.00 (Includes Motor)

A Machine for Stirring and
Dispensing Maple Sugar
Stainless Steel Parts
Motor Driven
$425.00 (Includes Motor)

HOME MADE

CANDY BOXES

Size 7⅜ x 3⅞ x 1
each .27

Size 9½ x 5 1/4 x 1
each .35

Packed 3 doz. to carton
Lots of 1000 printed your name FREE
Allow 3 weeks for printing

PLASTIC BOXES
HINGED COVER
7 x 3½ x 9 16" .... ea. .40
10 x 3½ x ⁵⁄₈" .... ea. .55
WHITE CARDBOARD WITH CELLO WINDOW TOP
3-1/2" x 2-1/2" x 3 4" — .08

White Round Plastic with
Transparent Cover
6" diameter, 1" deep.
Lots of 1000 - .30 ea.   Each - .35
7½" with 6 compartments
Each .45

PLASTIC CONTAINERS
for
Maple Cream
(Plain 48mm lids)
Holds 8 oz. (24 pak)
Doz. **$1.45**

Very Popular
PLASTIC
(Squeeze)
BOTTLES
We can supply this
item printed with your
name. Lots of 1000.
(Screen printed)

Half Pint
Complete with Cap
and Tip.
24 to Carton
$2.40 per doz.
Inquire about
Larger Quantities.

We have labels to fit.
Wrap around style
$5.00 per 100
Printed free in 1000 lots.

**CANDY CUPS FOR PACKING
YOUR MAPLE SUGAR CANDIES**

Colors - White, chocolate or red.

$1.50 per box of 500

WHITE ONE PIECE FOLDING BOXES

Two sizes—
6½ x 3½ x 2½ and 8-3/4 x 3-3/4 x 2-3/8
Comes folded flat - quickly becomes a neat
box. Sm. size **$1.25** doz. Lg. size **$1.50** doz.

SHREDDED CELLOPHANE — For attractive packaging
Choice of red, gold, green — List 2nd choice too.
Box of 10 pounds · **$15.00**

PADDED CUSHION PAPER IN ROLLS
12" wide and perforated every 15". **$50.00** per 250 ft. roll.
Excellent for packing fragile items such as pottery or glass.

Small Paper Sample Cups — Per 100 .... .75

**BEAUTIFULLY
LITHOGRAPHED
MAPLE PRODUCTS
TINS**

(Maple scene different than shown here.)

One pound size, holds 10 oz. small cakes........... **$ .45**
Two pound size, holds 1 lb. small cakes........... .55
Five pound size, holds 3 lb. small cakes........... .65

**OLD FASHIONED SUGAR
BUCKET with COVER**

Holds 1 lb.
Small
Sugar Cakes.

$4.50 each
Write for quantity prices

**STAINLESS
STEEL
FUNNEL FOR
FILLING CANDY
MOLDS**
Each **$12.00**

CANDY POURING DIPPER

Richards design, stainless steel
— about 1½ quarts with right
or left pouring lips, has sturdy
handle.   **$18.00**

— Scene at the Festival —

SUGAR CAMP ACCESSORIES

Flue Brush - Top side - Long handle - Nylon	$ 5.00
Flue Brushes, Bronze	10.95
Flue Brushes, Steel, threaded for 1/4" pipe	4.50

Top side Flu Brush 3.00

Grates — (State size and make of Evaporator)
Smoke Stack, all sizes — State size and make of Evaporator
Smoke Stack Covers, State size stack. (See page 6)

Vermont Evaporator Supplies

Draw off Faucets			$ 5.50
Floats, Copper			20.00
Regulators	Large $16.50	Small	15.50
Regulator Elbow	Large 14.00	Small	12.00
Gaskets	Large .30	Small	.25
Brass Plugs	Large 7.50	Small	5.75
Tin Plugs (for new style pans)			4.75
Hose Connection for new style pans		ea.	2.00
Clamps for above — Stainless Steel		ea.	.90

Check with us for Grimm, Leader, King, parts and supplies.

Scoops - Tin	$ 9.25
Scoops - Stainless steel	11.00
Skimmers - Tin	11.25
Skimmers - Stainless steel	13.50
Smaller size - Tin	7.00
Smaller size - St. steel	9.00

U Connections (two sizes for Vermonts - brass) $10.50 — $15.50
New flexible rubber U connections (no leaking - for old style)
Complete with clamps **Each (small) $3.75 — (large) $4.75**

Rubber Hose 3/4"	per ft.	$ 1.25
Rubber Hose 1"	per ft.	1.75
Rubber Hose 1¼"	per ft.	2.50

Rubber Hose 1½"	per ft.	2.75
Rubber Hose 2" wire reinforced	per ft.	5.00
6 foot length with 2" Brass Coupling		35.00
(Screws onto 2" tank nipple)		
Draw-off Gate 3/4" Regular iron		6.50
Draw-off Gate 1" Regular iron		7.25
Draw-off Gate 2" (Barrel size) Regular iron		10.50
Arch Paint (black)	per gallon	7.00
Lever action Brass Valve or Gate ½"		7.00
Lever action Brass Valve or Gate 3/4"		9.95
Lever action Brass Valve or Gate 1"		12.75

ALUMINUM PAINT — The same paint we have sold for years — but changes in government regulations require that we not label it for specific use in coating sap containers   Quart - **$4.00**   Gallon - **$12.00**

CISTERN PAINT for concrete. Smooth and sanitary. Approved by Food Authorities. 15# covers approx. 100 sq. ft. 2 coats .... per lb.   .75

Chrome No-Drip Faucets for filling bottles or cans. (Remember No Drip)

3/8" size	$21.00
with Union Shank	33.00
3/4" size	25.50
with Union Shank	38.50

1978 CATALOG

MAPLE SYRUP MAKING EQUIPMENT

REYNOLDS SUGAR BUSH

PHONE (A.C. 715) 449-2057 or 449-2536
ANIWA, WISCONSIN 54408

All prices herein are subject to change without notice!

Be sure and use your zip code when writing

Note Page 14
Describing the New
Maple Syrup Cans.

4

Backyard
Maple Syrup

Robert R. Morrow of Cornell University is distinguished not
only by his expertise in the maple syrup field, but also by his
ability to communicate his knowledge to others. From among
his various papers I have chosen to reprint, with permission,
the joint paper of Judy Yager and Robert R. Morrow issued in
1976 entitled "Home Maple Sirup Production."* The three
small photographs are from Leaflet 13, reprinted February
1975, also from the Department of Natural Resources at Cornell University.

Home Maple Sirup Production

Home maple sirup production is a feasible operation
for anyone with an interest and a desire to work. The

*I've tried several times to find out why New Yorkers insist upon the
spelling *sirup* and have so far managed only to discover that they do
insist upon it.

sirup produced may not always be light amber, but it is home-made which makes it special. With the listed equipment on hand, maple sirup making is not only fun but relatively easy.

Equipment for 15–20 taps, 5–10 gallons of sirup (1976 prices)

Investment

Brace $11.25
Bit, $^{7}/_{16}''$ .... $ 2.50
Spiles
       plastic (for tubing) .... 20¢ each
       tees .... 10¢ each
       metal (for buckets) .... 30–40¢ each
Plastic tubing .... 6½¢/foot
Buckets (optional)
       2½ gal., metal .... $2.15 each
       3½ gal., metal .... $2.60 each
       4 gal., plastic .... $1.90 each
Sap holding can (garbage can),
       20 gal., plastic $7.50
Galvanized washtub, 20–30 gal. $8.00
       Sirup pan, English tin
       (optional, in place of washtub) $40–80
Wood, at least 1 cord (8'×4'×4')
Rayon pre-filter $4–5/dozen
Orlon filter (2'×2') (2) .... $4.75 each, or
       Cone-shaped (to fit pail) $7.75
Sirup holding can, 5–10 gal., plastic
       or metal $5.00

Have at Home

Hammer
Used containers (replace buckets)
Chlorox
Squeeze bottle
Candy thermometer
Canning jars
Used cinder blocks or discarded bricks and metal, rocks
      or stones (for outdoor fireplace)
Large pail (for sirup holding can)

The variety of containers that can be used instead of sap buckets. (Photo courtesy of Department of Natural Resources, Cornell University.)

ABOUT 40 GAL. SAP PER GAL. SIRUP
ONE TAP YIELDS 10–15 GAL. SAP YEARLY
THREE TAPS NEEDED FOR ONE GAL. SIRUP

Inquire of neighboring producers for maple equipment. They may have extra equipment on hand or can include your needs in their orders. However, be sure to arrange for equipment in the fall or earlier. Spring is too late.

Some equipment can be purchased directly in local hardware or farm stores. Their prices tend to be expensive.

Maple dealers in central New York include H. W. Cook and R. M. Lamb. Cook sells a wide range of equipment to maple producers while Lamb specializes in plastic tube equipment. For the small operator, he has a special 20-spile kit with 500 feet of tubing. Maple dealers tend to sell in relatively large quantities. For only a half dozen spiles, for example, it is better to combine your order with that of your neighbor. Addresses follow:

H. W. Cook
Farm Service, Inc.
DeRuyter, New York 13052

R. M. Lamb
P.O. Box 368
Bernhards Bay, New York 13028

Used or obsolete stainless steel equipment can occasionally be purchased at greatly reduced prices from dairy farmers or milk processing plants. If the right size and shape, a good evaporator could result.

Choose the maple trees with care. Sugar or hard maple is superior and large open trees are ideal as the sugar content is usually higher and they produce more sap. Don't tap trees less than 10″ in diameter. Ease in collecting should also be considered.

Drill holes 2″ deep on a slant to facilitate sap drainage. The taphole should be rinsed with a solution of chlorox in water (1:10), using an old detergent squeeze bottle. The spile is then tapped in with a hammer until a snug fit prevents leakage. Metal spiles are needed for hanging buckets or pails, while plastic spiles and tees are designed for tubing.

Collect the sap every day or so as it spoils easily. With buckets, covers are preferred to keep out leaves, twigs and other debris. Home containers, used for buckets, need a hole punched near the top in order to hang on the spile. Empty the sap from each bucket into the washtub for boiling or a storage container for temporary storing.

If the trees are within 30′ of each other, plastic tubing can be used to join the trees so the sap will flow downhill to the collecting container. If the trees are farther apart, or if there is no slope, it may be better to have individual containers for each tree. Plastic tubes are cleaner than buckets and save labor in collecting. A second holding can for sap may be needed with more than 10 taps. Sap holding cans should have a total capacity of 2 gallons per taphole. A gallon a tap is a good daily flow, but occasionally double this amount may flow.

Most boiling should occur outside as the steam can be destructive to inside walls. A fireplace of cinder blocks or other materials can be built in a protected place that still has enough draft. A low retaining wall from an old building can provide protection from cold winds that otherwise might keep the fire too cool. The structure is flexible enough so that blocks can be moved around in order to take advantage of the wind for draft. A washtub, containing the boiling sap, is set over the fireplace or arch.

A collecting station using plastic tubing. (Photo courtesy of Department of Natural Resources, Cornell University.)

A backyard boiling setup with cinder block fireplace and washtub. (Photo courtesy of Department of Natural Resources, Cornell University.)

Cleaner sirup may be made from more expensive English tin pans, but many people have been satisfied with the home-made product from the galvanized washtub.

When boiling, it is handy to have a piece of sheet metal to protect the tub from rain and to cover it when warming the sap initially. Be sure the cover is not a smoke trap, though, as it will yield a smoky sirup. Sheet metal can also be used to partially shield against cold winds.

The amount of wood for burning is highly variable depending on the type of wood, how well seasoned, and how dry. It should be kept in mind that a home-made evaporator is usually not efficient and a great deal of heat is lost. Wood dried at least a year is preferable. Small, split wood is better than large chunks. Wood chips are more efficient to burn and can be mixed with larger wood or used separately. Chips or even sawdust can increase the boiling rate when the sap nears the sirup stage. Fast boiling at this time helps retain a lighter color and more maple flavor.

When the sap is close to being sirup (90–95 percent of water evaporated), it should be drained and finished in the kitchen. If left in the large tub, more sap must be added to the thickened solution, resulting in darker sirup with more caramelization. Finishing involves boiling until about 7¼ degrees above the boiling point of water, as determined by a candy thermometer. For more accuracy you can boil a pot of water to calibrate the exact boiling temperature which changes with barometric pressure.

Many homemakers do not recognize the sugar sand that settles out in the bottom of containers or occasionally causes cloudy sirup. To remove, filter the hot sirup (the hotter, the better) through a rayon pre-filter and the orlon filter. The pre-filter takes out most of the sand or sludge. Home cloths can also be used, but with less efficiency and the danger of imparting off-flavors or dyes. Also the sirup can simply be allowed to stand overnight while most of the sand settles to the bottom. Clear sirup can then be decanted off. Good filters are inexpensive, however, and improved sirup quality make them a good investment. After filtering, pour the hot sirup in canning jars, seal, and it's done.

Microorganisms build up during the season especially with the coming of warmer weather. They can

Filtering the syrup. (Photo courtesy of Tim Jardine, *Harbor Light,* Harbor Springs, Michigan.)

spoil the sap and degrade the sirup. Diluted chlorox is good for cleaning equipment, as residues are removed in boiling. Avoid other detergents. Tapholes can again be squirted with the chlorox solution (1:10) after midseason, while all buckets, containers, and tubs can be scrubbed with hot water as needed. Plastic tubing can wait until season's end for cleaning. Most important, don't let the sap stand around in warm weather—evaporate it to sirup.

When you have enough sirup, or it becomes too dark or poorly flavored, thoroughly clean and store all equipment. The sooner done, the easier to clean. Hot water is best, but the chlorox solution (1:10) is helpful for tubing. Store in a clean, dry place. Plastic tubing should be stored in containers that protect it from mice or other rodents.

Do not attempt to clean or plug the old tap hole. In a healthy tree new wood will enclose it within two to four years.

Judy Yager and Robert R. Morrow
Department of Natural Resources
Cornell University, 1976

We know now that we can make some respectable, desirable maple syrup at little or no cost. Consider then a quotation from Michigan State University's Extension Bulletin E-703: "Maple syrup and sugar is one agricultural crop in which there is no surplus. In fact, demand far exceeds available supply. The industry is not expanding, even though less than one percent of the potential resource is being used."

We will reserve consideration of the "big-business" aspects of maple-syrup production for a later chapter. For now, the following paper, previously unpublished, by Richard Lamore, will give you a good starting point for judging how large your own home operation should be.

COSTS AND PRODUCTIONS
of
SMALL MAPLE OPERATIONS

In Service Working Papers

prepared by
RICHARD LAMORE

Northeastern Forest Experiment Station
Forest Service, U.S. Department of Agriculture
Burlington, Vermont 05401, U.S.A.
November 9, 1976

Procedure for setting up a maple operation

Sugaring, as it is called, is a lot of hard work, but very rewarding and enjoyed by thousands of families, from Maine to Wisconsin.

I. First of all, you need some maple trees. These trees can be either sugar or red maple. If you have the trees, then you must estimate the number of potential taps. Trees that are 10″ to 14″ in diameter at breast height (approximately 4½′ from the ground level) are good for one tap. Trees from 15″ to 19″ in diameter are good for two taps, and trees 20″ to 24″ are good for three taps.

II. After you know what you have for taps, you can start looking around for some equipment. Good used equipment is okay; new equipment (Table 3–1) can be expensive. Places to check are: a) local maple producers for used equipment; b) hardware and farm supply stores, and c) the several companies in the area that manufacture the equipment, for new equipment.

Equipment Costs of Setting Up Three Small Maple Operations

General Equipment	Operation #1 Under 20 Taps	Operation #2 50–75 Taps	Operation #3 75–220 Taps
Evaporator	$ 65.00	$ 525.00	$ 795.00
Buckets/15 qt. @ $2.50 ea.	50.00	187.50	550.00
Covers @ $.71 ea.	14.20	53.25	156.00
Spouts @ $.28 ea.	5.60	21.00	62.00
Scoop	7.00	7.00	7.00
Skimmer	7.50	7.50	7.50
Bit brace & bit	7.50	7.00	7.00
Storage tank	10.00	100.00	150.00
Gathering pail	15.00	15.00	30.00
Gathering tank	—	160.00 (3BBL)	170.00 (4BBL)
Syrup thermometer	7.50	7.50	7.50
Dial thermometer	—	—	20.00
Syrup hydrometer/cup	10.00	10.00	10.00
Sap & syrup filters	8.00	12.00	20.00
Filter tank	5.00	15.00	51.00
Syrup grading set	3.75	3.75	3.75
Total investment	$215.50	$1,131.50	$2,046.75
Cost per tap	$ 10.78	$ 15.09	$ 9.30

III. If you are planning to burn wood in your evaporator, you should have good dry hardwood whenever possible. It takes approximately one cord (4'×4'×8') to make approximately 28 gallons of syrup.

IV. You should begin tapping about the first of March. In this area of Vermont you can expect to have good sap flows from the first of March until around the 15th of April. A 2½" to 3" tap hole, $^7/_{16}$" in diameter, in good sound wood is sufficient.

V. Sap should be gathered daily when the trees are running, and boiled down as soon as possible. Warm or old sap can result in poor quality syrup.

Filtering sugar sand from covered evaporators. (Photo courtesy of Dick Smith.)

VI.   When boiling sap down to syrup, one must calibrate his candy or syrup thermometers each day and adjust them to the boiling point of water. When your sap reaches 7° above the boiling point of water, you have syrup. At this point, you should draw off the syrup and, while it is still hot, put it through a clean felt or wool filter. This process takes the "sugar sand" out of your syrup and eliminates sediment in the finished product.

VII.   Syrup should be 180°F when you can it, and you should fill your containers enough so as to leave little or no air space. Syrup to be sold in Vermont must be color-graded, and containers labeled with grade and of proper density (weight), which is measured by your syrup hydrometer; 59°Brix for hot syrup (211°F) or 65.46°Brix at room temperature (68°F). If your syrup is too thin or too light, it will spoil easily; if it is too thick, it will crystalize. A gallon of maple syrup will weigh 11 pounds.

Syrup productions and returns

Operation size #1 production on an average year with 2.5 sap (state average): you would produce approximately five gallons of syrup. If you normally buy three or four gallons of syrup a year for household use and gifts, it would take you approximately four seasons to pay for your operation.

Operation size #2 with 50–75 taps: you can expect a syrup production of 14 to 20 gallons on an average year. On this size operation you will have to be prepared to handle approximately 750 gallons of sap during the sugar season. Because of this, the initial cost of your operation is considerably higher than operation size #1, due to the fact that a complete arch-type evaporator is needed. A 2'×4' evaporator is adequate for this size operation. It boils off approximately 15 gallons of sap per hour. If you made 20 gallons a season and sold 16 gallons at $11.00 each, it would take you approximately 6½ seasons to pay for your operation.

Operation size #3 with 75–220 taps: your syrup production per season would be 20 to 64 gallons. Again,

This homemade evaporator for box elder sap produced 5 gallons of top-grade syrup in 1978. (Photo courtesy of Dick Hakes.)

like operation size #2, you will need a full size arch-type evaporator; in this case a 2′×6′ rig is adequate. It boils off approximately 32 gallons of sap per hour, which means nearly a gallon of finished syrup per hour, with average 2.5 sap. If you sold 45 gallons of each season's production at $11.00 a gallon, it would take you 4 years to pay for your operation.

Thus far, you are a moonshiner, your product—untaxed, unstamped, uninspected and unreported—is of substantial value, and the profit to your purse and your soul is really all clear and keepable. When you get bigger, the problems begin.

The most important requirement for the production of maple syrup—one not mentioned by any of the authorities and experts—is the mutual desire of men and women, husbands and wives or whomever, to make the project succeed. Occasionally a male college professor, for example, will run a successful mini-operation during his spring vacation, but almost always the successful operation calls for a joint effort by a man and a woman, and possibly their children, and a dedication to sharing the work and the fun and the challenges.

NOTE: To realize the gratification people feel in the spring rite of tapping maple trees you should attend, if possible, one of the many maple festivals held throughout the country. A young woman recently said to me, "I was never so happy when as a child we went to the Sugar Festival at Shepherd, Michigan, and had maple taffy off the snow." And a young doctor recalled as a highlight of his college experience the weekend when his class attended the Geauga County Maple Festival and visited a sugar house operating out of Chardon, Ohio. Burton, Ohio, by the way, has the only municipally owned and operated sugar camp in North America.

5

Almost Everything You Need to Know in Only Six Pages

There are so many thousands of pages of information on maples, most of it trifling and irrelevant, that I found it impossible to synthesize and extract the material which will be most useful for you. A few facts and opinions you may find helpful are listed below. Special subjects will be covered in the appendix listing sources which I've found useful and to which you may write for more information.

1. *Tap holes:* The standard recommended rate per tree is:

Tree Diameter at Breast Height (in Inches)	No. of Tap Holes
10–17	1
17–24	2
24–30	3
30 and over	4

2. *When to tap:* Sap flow begins when thawing starts and quits when freezing ends. Fall tapping is *not* recommended, though possible.

3. *Rate of flow:* Up to ½ gallon per hour per tap hole; 4 to 80 gallons per tap hole per season, but probably 5 to 15 gallons with an average of about 9 gallons of sap per season. The earliest sap is the clearest and most highly prized for syrup making.

Using a power drill to make holes for gathering maple sap. (Photo courtesy of Dick Smith.)

4. *Labor:* Two men can hand tap and hang from 500 to 600 buckets a day, and nearly twice that with a power tapper.

5. *Tap holes per acre:* 70 to 90 per acre (43,560 square feet) to yield 15 to 25 gallons of syrup. 150 tap holes per acre assumes large trees with no room for small ones to eventually replace them.

6. *Sugar content of sap:* Sugar content of sap of individual trees tends to run from 1.5% to 4.1%, with an average of about 2½%, but a few trees, though I do not know of their location, have been reported with sugar contents of 9% and even 11%. Incredible? Not really. The sucrose in sugar cane runs between 16 and 17% and in sugar beets about 18%. Divide the percentage of sugar content of the sap into 86 to determine the number of gallons of sap required to produce one gallon of syrup. 2.2% sugar in the sap, divided into 86, equals 40 gallons needed for one gallon of syrup. One gallon of syrup will make 6½ to 9 pounds of sugar.

7. *Labor requirements for the tap holes:* Anywhere from one man for 150 buckets to one man for 3,000 tap holes with a pump and plastic tubing system.

9. *Sap characteristics:* It freezes, like water. It tastes "buddy" with the onset of buds on the trees, and the tapping is then discontinued.

10. *Collecting tanks:* The capacity of tanks is rated in barrels. One barrel equals 32 gallons. Three to five barrel tanks may be horsedrawn, but larger numbers require a tracter or equivalent, which can hold sap until it is evaporated. One barrel capacity is estimated to be needed for every 50 tap holes.

11. *Storage tanks:* Tanks used for sap storage at the evaporation site may range from the plastic garbage can of the backyard operation to several thousand-gallon tanks.

12. *Evaporator houses:* If you have fewer than 220 taps you may be able to get by without a special evaporator house, but more taps than that will require an

Oxen-drawn collecting tank, Washington, New Hampshire. (Photo courtesy of Dick Smith.)

evaporator house for equipment storage, convenience and sanitation. Enforced health regulations could signal the closing of many older evaporator houses. Consult with the supplier of your evaporator and your extension director about your probable needs if you are in established maple country and plan on going beyond the country, backyard, mini-type operation.

13. *Fuel:* Fuel costs are about equal to labor costs in producing syrup, perhaps $2.00 a gallon for each. Oil is the most convenient fuel, but wood is probably more

reliable and can be much cheaper. One gallon of #2 fuel oil evaporates 10 to 12 gallons of sap to produce syrup. Three to four gallons of fuel oil produce one gallon of syrup. One cord of wood will boil off the production of about 75 taps, and will evaporate about as much as 175 gallons of oil can evaporate.

14. *Evaporation:* Check the boiling point of water with a thermometer first, and then proceed to evaporate

Skimming boiling syrup with a pan. (Photo courtesy of Tim Jardine, *Harbor Light,* Harbor Springs, Michigan.)

your sap. When the temperature of the boiling sap reaches exactly 7 degrees above the boiling point of water, it is ready to pour off and strain for syrup. When the temperature is raised to 40–45 degrees above the boiling point of water the sap may be removed from the heat, stirred until it begins to crystalize and stiffen, and poured into molds as very hard sugar candy. Boiled too little, syrup is watery and lacking flavor, but boiled too long it becomes sugary. Sap is skimmed when boiling. Care must be taken to avoid scorching the sap, and a bit of commercial sap defoamer might be used to prevent surging. For a complete description of the evaporation process (and an absolute requirement for anything larger than a backyard operation), read *Agricultural Handbook No. 134–Maple Sirup Producers Manual* (Superintendent of Documents, U.S. Printing Office, Washington D.C. 20402, $2.50).

15. *Packaging:* Any sterilized jug, jar or tin will suffice to hold your syrup, but the syrup should be above 180 degrees when poured into the container, which must be filled to the top and sealed. Never bottle cold syrup for shipment or for sale in stores. Keep open containers refrigerated.

6

Grades of Syrup

For many, many years, old-time producers of maple syrup have been jealous of their reputation for selling only the very finest syrup that could be made. Great care and attention were given to sanitation and proper evaporation by these men, and when they judged the product to be too dark or slightly off flavor, they would discontinue the operation. Their reputations, and the prices they commanded, were based on the finest flavor that could be obtained, and rightly so.

Recently, however, the demand for maple syrup has been so great that standards and requirements have been appreciably changed.

Old U.S. Standards (see p. 94 of *Agricultural Handbook No. 134* for full requirements):
U.S. Grade AA (Fancy)
U.S. Grade A
U.S. Grade B

New U.S. Standards:
>Grade A Light Amber
>Grade A Medium Amber
>Grade A Dark Amber
>Grade B or Utility
>Grade C or Unclassified

Canadian Grades
>Canada Fancy—very light amber, mild characteristic flavor
>Canada Light—light amber, mild, characteristic flavor
>Canada Medium—dark amber, stronger, characteristic flavor
>Canada Dark—dark, stronger, characteristic flavor, but may have a trace of fermentation

Wisconsin Grades
>Wisconsin Fancy
>Wisconsin Grade A
>Wisconsin Manufacturers Grade

Check with your label supplier before labeling your product for general distribution. Conscience and quality dictate the reputations of the smaller syrup producers, but larger producers will find substantial disagreement among themselves about standards, labeling and enforcement. Someone said of whiskey that it's all good, but some kinds are better than others. And so it is with maple syrup.

Experience and mistakes are the only instructors for making "better" maple syrup.

7

Prices

Maple syrup prices have tended to follow general consumer price indexes in the past. The trend will probably continue in the future if the product is carefully marketed, and if it isn't adulterated, misrepresented or debased.

A few examples:

One charming mail order folder includes this description of "Vermont Best Grade Syrup": "We call our syrup best grade because it is much more nutritious than the fancier types. Very rarely seen out of Vermont. We Vermonters use all of it. Rich nutlike flavor. 1 qt. $7.50 plus $1.25 postage."

A local health food store is selling Pure Maple Syrup—Grade A Dark Amber, producer and packager unknown, for $6.59 per quart. Recently Eastern sugar houses quoted prices for Grade A Pure Maple Syrup at from $12.00 to $21.50 per gallon F.O.B. One mail order producer quoted Fancy at $14.50, Grade A at $14.00, Grade B at $13.50 and Grade C at $10.00.

The price range for Hard Cake Maple Sugar ran from $2.00 to $4.75 per pound F.O.B.

An "imitation maple flavor" I recently purchased for 49¢ an ounce contained, according to the label, water, caramel color, alcohol, fenugreek, vanilla extract, coffee and other natural extractives, propylene glycol and ethyl vanillin.

Before judging imitation maple syrup flavoring, consider the story of Lt. Al Schneider: "Ours was a mule-carrying detached artillery outfit in Burma at Christmastime 1944, and the only present that had gotten through was a bottle of imitation maple my wife had sent me. We cut a steel plate off a Japanese tank, the cook whipped together a mess of pancakes, and we had a real American Christmas dinner with that stretched maple flavor. It took a lot of wood."

Closer to the natural product, but still some distance removed from the original blend Patrick James Towle formulated in 1899 of cane and maple syrups only, is Towles Log

Lt. Al Schneider's Burmese maple pancakes.

Cabin Syrup. According to its label it contains 59.% sugar syrup, 37.7% corn syrup, 3.0% maple sugar syrup, artificial flavor, sodium benzoate and sorbic acid (preservatives) and caramel color. The original product was packaged in an attractive log cabin–shaped tin container inspired by the shape of Lincoln's early home. It gave midwesterners the taste of maple and a wholesome, natural sweetener at a price they could afford, and the Towles' log cabin at one time graced a host of breakfast tables. The success of the product attracted the atention of a major corporation, and the business was sold to it by the Towles in 1928. Many of us would give a great deal to have the original old-fashioned blend back in the tin log cabin again.

Since the name *maple* has economic value, by law any blend using the name *maple* must contain at least 2% pure maple syrup. There is nothing inherently wrong with blends; accordingly, major blenders are estimated to be using 10% to 15% of the total U.S. production of pure syrup in making blends. The natural maple flavor is unique and much desired in a wide variety of foods, and with cane and beet sugar in surplus supply and selling for as low as 8¢ a pound on the world market it is not surprising that people are attracted to good, economical maple blends.

Maple's main competition as a sweetener may, in the future, come not from cane or beet sugar, but from such darlings of the dentists as monellin, xylitol, aspartame, the dihydrochalcones from citrus peels, and miraculin. They are intense sweeteners, but not foods.

About twenty years ago some producers of sap decided that there was merit in having a single efficient evaporator run by an expert to which producers would haul their sap, much like old-fashioned creameries, rather than a number of relatively small and inefficient evaporators. Some co-ops work quite well for their members, and in other cases it proves more satisfactory for all concerned to let an individual run the central evaporator on his own account. For the general assistance of both buyers and sellers of sap, the *National Maple Syrup Digest* publishes anticipated prices for the coming months. The information below is from their article on page 6 of the February 1978 issue.

Sap prices

Each year, in the February issue, we publish a chart of the sap prices paid by one New York Producer for the past two years and the proposed price to be paid in the coming season along with the respective retail and wholesale price of syrup in consumer packages.

Please remember, this chart is published to be used only as a guide and the Digest in no way intends that it should dictate the price paid for sap by any producer.

Year	1976–77	1978
Retail	14.00	15.00
Wholesale	10.60	11.40
Sap Brix	per gal.	per gal.
1.5	.028	0.18
1.6	.039	.041
1.7	.050	.054
1.8	.061	.065
1.9	.071	.076
2.0	.08	.085
2.1	.088	.093
2.2	.095	.101
2.3	.102	.108
2.4	.108	.114
2.5	.114	.121
2.6	.120	.128
2.7	.126	.135
2.8	.132	.141
2.9	.138	.147
3.0	.144	.153
3.1	.150	.159
3.2	.156	.165
3.3	.162	.171
3.4	.168	.177
3.5	.174	.183
3.6	.180	.189
3.7	.185	.195
3.8	.191	.201
3.9	.196	.207
4.0	.202	.212

Some operators are using their skills to cook delicious homemade jellies and jams for marketing when the syrup season is over. And a few syrup makers have found it helpful to supplement their incomes with produce from greenhouses and gardens, plus sales of evergreen wreathes and gift boxes for the Christmas holidays. Nobody is promising that syrup production will make a millionaire of you, or that you will become a skilled syrup maker overnight. But whatever you need to do to make a go of your maple enterprise, the proper dedication and pioneering spirit can make it all worthwhile.

8

Maple as a Business

While there are thousands of men and women who make a very satisfactory living in the maple business, there are thousands more who have abandoned the sugar bush for the myriad opportunities of the city. When maple syrup production is considered a business rather than a hobby, a commitment must be made to living in either the country or a small town in the country. As in any land-based enterprise, your ultimate success will depend on patience and an inherent cheerfulness in the face of adversity. The maple business is not a "get-rich-quick" undertaking. But assuming you are generally cheerful and healthy, and reasonably patient, I know of no other farming–retailing endeavour that offers so much and requires, comparatively, so little

At the end of this chapter is a copy of the *In Service Working Papers* prepared by Neil K. Huyler of the Northeastern Forest Experiment Station. You will note that the estimated cost per season for a 3,000-tap operation is $6,270, or roughly one-fourth what it costs today for a single 120-horsepower tractor.

Add a few more tractors, plows, discs, combines and the rest, and it quickly becomes clear that entry into the grain farming business can easily run into a cost of $100,000. The person setting up a maple operation must somehow acquire a modest amount of land, buildings and equipment, but here too the investment is much less than it would be for a commercial grain farming, livestock or poultry enterprise.

The net return from a 3,000-tap operation may look rather small considering the planning and effort it requires, but you should remember that this is the result of only a few months' work in the spring, that the product is sold at wholesale, and that much larger mapling operations are always very feasible.

From the records I have been able to obtain, it seems many families have made a nice living with from 500 to 1500 taps, doing the work themselves and supplementing their income by raising chickens, cows, hogs, goats, dogs or whatnot. Dependable outside help will probably be needed during the rush for from 1,700 to 4,200 taps, plus an extra source of income on the side. But when the number of taps is above 4,200, a rather nice business can be developed on a full-time, year-around basis if you sell your sap by mail order at retail prices of your own fixing. One operator I know is selling ½ pints for $3.50, pints for $5, quarts for $8 and ½ gallons for $13 plus 10% postage. This year he made 840 gallons from 4500 taps.

Further up the scale is a family operation, reported in the December 1973 issue of the *Maple Syrup Digest*, which sold 4,200 gallons of syrup, using over 40 miles of plastic tubing for gathering the sap. Few of us, however, could match them for industry no matter how large the family: they also produced and sold 25,000 board feet of lumber, plus 200 cords of firewood, plus 500 tons of hay.

At the top of the scale, one operator tried to handle 40,000 taps and failed. But on the other hand, a small family corporation runs 35,000 taps of its own, buys the production from 75,000 taps handled by others, and runs a retail supply business in addition.

Once you've decided to make maplin' your business, I strongly urge you to get the latest cost-return figures available from Michigan, New York and Vermont, and then to decide how much work you really care to do, how much management ability you have, and what the alternatives are for you. There is no particular hurry. It isn't like missing out on a once-in-a-lifetime McDonald franchise. But if you're sold on the idea, you should first pin down the location you feel is ideal. I know hundreds of millionaire farmers who started out as tenants on a shoestring; they knew what they wanted and were willing to pay the price in labor, patience and fortitude.

Though we've only talked about maple syrup and sugar so far, it should never be forgotten that the maple tree is always in strong demand for lumber and firewood as well. Year after year these trees keep growing, no matter what the state of the nation or the world. Someday you should harvest a few. I personally would rather have a growing tree than gold and silver in a vault. The government doesn't tax you for capital gains while the trees grow, and it probably won't confiscate your trees the way it could, in one way or another, expropriate many other kinds of tangibles.

There are no guarantees on anything anymore. But for those who really enjoy the business, owning and harvesting maples looks like as sound and secure an investment as anything else, and much, much better than many.

Example of Cost Estimates Prepared for Release to Individual Producers

1976 Update
In Service Working Papers
prepared by
Neil K. Huyler
Forest Products Technologist
Maple Products Marketing Project
Northeastern Forest Experiment Station
P.O. Box 968, 705 Spear Street
Burlington, VT 05401

Cost of Tubing System (Woods Operation)

The total investment cost for a 3,000-tap tubing with vacuum system comes to about $6,270. This figures to be about $2.09 per tap. The cost break-down for the 3,000 tap operation is as follows:

Item	Cost/Tap	Total Cost
Spouts	$ .20	$ 600
Tubing ⁵/₁₆" @ 13 feet/tap@ 5¢/foot	.65	1,950
½" conduit @ 2 feet/tap (mainline)	.18	540
¾" conduit @ 1.2 feet/tap (mainline)	13	396
1" conduit @ .7 feet/tap (mainline)	.16	480
Tees—⁵/₁₆"	.10	300
Large tees	.006	18
Connectors—⁵/₁₆"	.01	30
4 way-wyes	.012	36
Spring clips—large & small	.01	30
Miscellaneous small items (hammers, pliers, knives, etc.)	.02	60
Storage tanks (2 35-BBL tanks)	.22	750
Power tapper	.06	180
Materials (coding tags, paint & sprayer, gas, hammers, pliers, etc.)	.083	250
TOTAL	$1.87	$5,620
Optional: Pump and tank for vacuum	$2.09	$6,270

Annual Cost (Woods Operation)

This is assuming a 10-year depreciation on equipment and 10 percent interest on investment.

[1]Optimum size or least cost operation.

Annual Cost	Dollar/Tap	Total Cost
Rental value of orchard	$ .11	$ 330
Capital cost (equipment)	.34	1,020
Material cost	.08	250
Labor @ $2.25/hour avg. 9.6 man,min./tap	.36	1,080
TOTAL ANNUAL COST	$ .89	$2.680

$$\text{Cost/gal. of sirup} = \frac{\$2,680}{750 \text{ gal. sirup}^2} = \$3.57$$

Cost of Manufacturing (Processing Operation)

The following are estimates of major equipment cost for processing sap to sirup.

Quantity	Item	Total Cost
1	6′×16′ complete evaporator × $4,221 (includes 2 10-gal./hr. oil burners × $832)	$5,053.00
	Bricking and installation costs	402.20
1	Fuel storage tank (1,000 gal. retail)	517.32
1	Sap storage tank (35-barrel tank)	375.00
1	Filter tank and racks (30 gal/cap.)	156.00
1	Automatic sirup drawoff	150.00
4	Synthetic filters	32.00
1	Sap hydrometer	4.50
1	Sirup hydrometer	4.50
	Gate valves, tees, pipe, etc.	25.00
1	Grading set	3.75
	Cleaning equipment	15.00
	TOTAL EQUIPMENT COST	$6,738.00
		$2.25/tap

Cost-Capital Investment for Processing

Capital Investment		Life/Yrs.	Annual Cost[3]
Land	$1,000		
Building	1,560	25	$171.91
Plant Equip.	6,738	20	791.72
TOTAL	$9,298		$963.63

[2] Assuming a yield of 1 quart of sirup per tap.
[3] Depreciation and 10 percent interest on investment.

Annual Cost (Processing)

Capital cost	$ 963.63
Labor (hired) @ $3.00/hr.	400.00
Fuel (oil & gas) @ 40¢/gal.	1,050.00
Electricity	50.00
TOTAL ANNUAL COST	$2,463.63

$$\text{Cost/gal. of sirup} = \frac{\$2,463.63}{750 \text{ gal. sirup}} = \$3.29$$

Cost Summary (Tubing System)

	Per Tap	Per Gal. Sirup
Woods operation	$ .89	$3.57
Processing operation	.82	3.29
TOTAL COST	$1.71	$6.86

Income Statement (Tubing System)

Bulk Sales Income: Per Gallon

90 percent Grade A and Fancy @ 80¢/lb. − $8.80/gal. =	$7.92
10 percent Grade B and lower @ 60¢/lb. − $6.60/gal. =	.66
TOTAL AVERAGE PRICE	$8.58
Less production cost	6.86
Return to operator and management	$1.72

Cost of Bucket Operation (Woods Operation)

The total investment cost for a 3,000-tap bucket operation comes to about $13,170. This figures to be about $4.39 per tap for the initial investment cost. The cost break-down is as follows:

Item	Cost/Tap	Total Cost
Bucket, spouts, and covers	$3.44	$10,320
Tractor[4] and sap sled	.40	1,200
Materials	.10	300
Hand tools including power tappers	.133	400
Sap storage tanks (2 35-BBL tanks)	.25	750
Bucket washer	.067	200
TOTAL	$4.39	$13,170

[4]Tractor cost @ $3.50/hr. (depreciation, fuel, interest, housing, etc.).

Annual Cost (Woods Operation for Buckets)

This is assuming a 30-year depreciation rate on the buckets, spouts, covers, etc. and 10 percent interest on investment.

Annual Cost	Dollar/Tap	Total Cost
Capital cost (equipment)	$ .47	$1,397
Rental value of orchard	.11	330
Materials	.10	300
Labor @ $2.25/hour avg. 12.3 man min./tap	.46	1,384
TOTAL ANNUAL COST	$1.14	$3,411

$$\text{Cost/gal. of sirup} = \frac{\$3,411}{750 \text{ gal. sirup}^5} = \$4.55$$

Annual Cost (Processing-Buckets)

Capital cost	$ 963.63
Labor (hired) @ $3.00/hr.	400.00
Fuel (oil & gas) @ 40¢/gal.	1,050.00
Electricity	50.00
TOTAL ANNUAL COST	$2,463.63

$$\text{Cost/gal. of sirup} = \frac{\$2,463.63}{750 \text{ gal. sirup}} = \$3.29$$

Cost Summary (Bucket System)

	Per Tap	Per Gal. Sirup
Woods operation	$1.14	$4.55
Processing operation	.82	3.29
TOTAL COST	$1.96	$7.84

Income Statement (Bucket System)

Bulk Sales Income: Per Gallon	
90 percent Grade A and Fancy @ 80¢/lb. − $8.80/gal. =	$7.92
10 percent Grade B and lower @ 60¢/lb. − $6.60/gal. =	.66
TOTAL AVERAGE PRICE/GAL.	$8.58
Less production cost	7.84
Return to operator and management	$ .74

[5] Assuming a yield of 1 quart per tap.

MAKING MAPLE SUGAR

9

History

When the Pilgrims landed on the New England coast in 1620, the diets of the local Indians contained no sugar, no salt, no milk and no alcoholic beverages. Even honey was missing, since our honey bee is a European import.

The absence of sugar was due to the fact that the principal item in the diet of the Indian was corn, and corn would not mature in the cooler areas where maple trees were most abundant. Dr. M. K. Bennett states in "The Food Economy of the New England Indians, 1605–75" that while the Indians of Maine and upper New York to the west and the upper St. Lawrence to the northeast did make a small amount of maple syrup and sugar in their earthen pots, none was made by the coastal Indians of eastern Connecticut, Rhode Island, central and eastern Massachusetts, New Hampshire and Maine. At that time, he says, "all of Vermont, the highlands covering most of New

Hampshire, and the western highlands of Massachusetts and Connecticut were apparently unoccupied."*

It was the iron kettle, which the Indians first attempted to steal from Champlain's men in 1605, and for which they were massacred, that was the key to immediate, near-universal usage of maple sugar by later Indians, colonists, farmers and pioneers. This trading item simplified the evaporation of sap in quantities adequate for the needs of all the frontier families.

From near-zero production of maple syrup and sugar in this country we find that by 1852, as indicated by the following report from the Farmers Club of the American Institute of the City of New York, practically everyone was making maple sweeteners for sale, for barter, and for their own use.

The report of the Farmers Club meeting held at Castle Garden, on March 1, 1853, reads, in part:†

"Farmer's Club, Tuesday, March 1st, 1853 Regular Meeting.

The Chairman stated the subject—The Forest Trees of America—and asked Mr. Nash if he had anything to remark on the subject. Alanson Nash, of New York, stated:

THE SUGAR MAPLE, OR ACER SACCHARINUM,
Is a tree that grows extensively in most parts of North America. It is a nobel, majestic tree, and one of the most useful and ornamental trees in America. . . . its great excellence consists in its furnishing a sap from which vast quantities of sugar are made during the months of February, March and April; an open winter, constantly freezing and thawing, is a forerunner of a good flowing of sap.

A grove of maple trees is almost equal, acre for acre, to the sugar cane, to produce sugar and molasses. We have seen fields of 200 to 300 acres set out with young shoots of the maple tree, and in a few years forming a thrifty growth. In fifteen years, a sapling taken from the

---

*M. K. Bennett, "The Food Economy of the New England Indians, 1605–75," *The Journal of Political Economy,* Vol. LXIII, No. 5, October 1955, p. 369–397.

†*Transactions of the American Institute of the City of New York for the year 1852, Albany,* Charles Van Benthuysen, Printer to the Legislature, 1853.

woods and transplanted, will afford a delicious shade for a dwelling. We have known this tree to grow 400 years in the forest, but generally it is a tree that rarely reaches the age of 300 years. The maple grows up quickly and in many parts of the United States the trees have come up as a second growth since the country has been cleared and settled, and now form excellent sugar groves, the most beautiful seen in our country.

The young trees yield the sap much more freely and in greater quantity than the old trees, but drawing the sap from young trees stops their growth, and in a few years will kill them. A tree ought to arrive at the age of fifty years before it is used for sugar. We have known full-grown trees to produce 500 quarts of sap in one season. From two to eight pounds of sugar a tree, is a good yield for a sugar grove in one season.

The flowing of the sap is influenced by the wind and weather; a southerly and westerly wind in a clear day will start a full flow of the sap, but a northeast wind of two hours' duration will stop the running of the sap, even when the temperature of the air is lowered but a very few degrees. . . .

Large and bushy trees that stand in the open grounds, insular, and in favorable situations for soil and light, sometimes yield great quantities of sap. It is said that a single tree has been known to furnish thirty gallons of sap in twenty-four consecutive hours; but this can only happen where the tree enjoys peculiar advantages for growth and location. The sap is a delicious drink; all animals are fond of it; it comes away from the tree as clear as crystal, but in twenty-four hours it will change its color, and in 48 hours begins to sour and put on more or less of the saccharine fermentation. It first grows of a brown color, then it becomes ropy and sour, and makes a mucilage like a clot in vinegar. It makes the best vinegar in the world.

The time for tapping trees to obtain sap is in February, March and April, but generally more sugar is made in the Northern States and Canada in April than in any other month. When the sprigs and limbs of the maple tree in February and March which have been broken by ice in the preceding winter exhibit signs of the sap dropping from them, the time to tap the tree for making sugar has

Checking the sap flow, Bartlett, New Hampshire. (Photo courtesy of Dick Smith.)

come. A two inch auger is bored into the tree three inches, at about two to three feet from the ground. Then a hollow spout or syphon of sumach is driven into the hole tight so as to prevent the sap leaking. Many sugar makers box the tree with an axe. Into this box a bit is passed to form a hole for a spout. This barbarous method destroys the growth of the tree. Clean pails or tubs of pine ought to be used to catch the sap when it runs. The sap ought to be caught every day and boiled.

There are many improved methods of making the sugar. We have seen maple sugar that would vie with the best loaf and lump sugar. Indeed maple sugar, when boiled clear, and while the sap is fresh from the tree, will usually granulate or crystalize superior to the sugar produced by the cane. Much depends on the skill and care of the operator in the yield of sugar obtained from a given quantity of sap. We have known a pound and a half of sugar obtained from ten quarts of sap, and at other times it would take twenty quarts to yield a pound.

The sap ought to be boiled down in a kettle set in an arch in the open air, to prevent ashes and other ingredients from falling into it.

The sugar will not granulate when the syrup or molasses is sour or burnt. As the molasses thickens it boils not unlike soap; then the fire must be slacked. The process ought to be conducted slowly. A few coals kept under the kettle will be quite sufficient to boil the sugar dry. A wooden paddle may be used to granulate the sugar, and this is done by constantly stirring the sugar when it crystalizes.

We have ascertained from the United States census for 1850, that there were produced in the United States in that year, 33,980,459 pounds of maple sugar, besides molasses, of which the several States furnished the following quantities of sugar:

	Pounds
Maine,	97,541
New Hampshire,	1,392,429
Massachusetts,	768,596
Vermont,	5,159,641
Connecticut,	37,781
New-York,	10,210,764

	Pounds
New-Jersey,	5,886
Pennsylvania,	2,218,641
Maryland,	47,740
Virginia,	1,223,905
North Carolina,	27,448
South Carolina,	200
Georgia,	50
Alabama,	473
Mississippi,	110
Louisiana,	8,825
Tennessee,	159,617
Kentucky,	388,525
Ohio,	4,428,648
Michigan,	2,423,897
Indiana,	2,921,638
Illinois,	246,078
Missouri,	171,642
Iowa,	70,684
Wisconsin,	661,969
Minnesota,	2,950
Total,	32,759,269

Rhode Island, Texas, Oregon, California, Utah, New Mexico, Delaware and Florida. These States and Territories are not returned, but there is returned 1,221,194 pounds overplus.

This does not include the amount of maple sugar made by the Indian population east of the Mississippi, which may be set down at 3,000,000 of pounds. For the Indian population west of the Mississippi and Lake Superior, say 2,000,000 of pounds. There was returned to the Census department of Canada in 1849, of maple sugar made in these provinces:

For Upper Canada, ... 4,160,667 pounds
For Lower Canada, ... 2,303,168 pounds

No returns in from Nova Scotia, or New Brunswick, Newfoundland and Labrador.

The above is independent of molasses made from maple sap, which may be set down at 20,000,000 of gallons annually made in North America. The world has seen but few trees of more importance than the maple.

The chairman said, that great improvements had been made in the manufacturing of maple sugar. He had seen at recent Fairs, specimens of it, which would lose nothing, when compared with Stuart's best refined loaf sugar.

Mr. Pike doubted whether the sugar maple yielded sap enough to be worth having at twenty-five years of age. He had them of that age, and they do not give sap worth the trouble of tapping the trees.

Mr. Nash.—The tree requires (for much sap) a cool, moist, rich soil; when transplanted to a dry one, it degenerates. It loves frosty ground, grows well and yields abundantly its sap. When taken to the southward it degenerates. It thrives northerly to Labrador and to Hudson's Bay. I never saw one growing in a swamp. It loves a clear mountainous country. When broken by ice or cut away by the axe, leave but one chief limb on the body, and it thrives. I think, by an electrical action.

Chairman.—It does best in Ohio and Kentucky, upon the flatlands of those States, where it grows in vast groves and forests.

Judge Van Wyck.—We have had a very important communication made to us to-day, by Counsellor Nash, on the produce of the *acer saccharinum,* or sugar maple of the United States. The statistics here given are taken from the latest and best sources at Washington, show clearly, the tree, for its prosperous growth requires a rich soil, and pretty high northern latitude. . . . As to the inducements of our people to preserve and increase the numbers of this valuable tree, they are many and strong. The sugar is more healthy, palatable and cleaner, than that made from the cane. The cane sugar of the United States is cleaner than the sugar of the West India islands and some other quarters. The market price is always a paying one—from 12 to 22 cents per pounds, according to quality. Much depends on the making, boiling, purifying and refining; if these are properly attended to, it can be made almost as white and beautiful as the best double-refined, made from the cane, and much more palatable and healthy. There is a peculiar flavor imparted to the maple sugar if properly manufactured, which no other plant producing the juice has. The produce of sap from different trees, is very different, some producing much more than others, according to location, size, thrift and manner of tapping. I have known trees to produce 6 or seven pails full in a day or 24 hours, others much less. A gentleman, a sugar manufacturer, in western New-York, writes: "Having introduced twenty tubes into a sugar maple, I drew from it in the same day 23 gallons, 3 quarts of sap, which gave 7½ lbs. of sugar; 33 pounds have been made this season from the same tree, which supposes 100 gallons of sap." It would seem from this, that only a little more than three gallons for a pound, though four are commonly allowed. The sugar maple thrives best when insulated, not near any other tree; high or low ground, if rich, and near moisture are best. Great havoc has been committed of late on the sugar, and all other kinds of the valuable tree; this for fuel, charcoal and potash, for all of which it is very fine; it contains a great deal of the alkaline principle, and of course produces pearlash in quantity and quality, greater and better than almost any other tree. The tree should be preserved with great care for timber, sugar and ornament, being as beautiful as useful." . . .

Mr. R. L. Pell added these remarks:

THE MAPLE, (Acer.)

This tree is justly held in very high estimation, particularly the bird's-eye which resembles a peacock's tail, and is extremely pretty. It is only the tops of old trees that take on these beautiful undulations, consequently the hard maple and the bird's-eye are synonymous; they are produced from seeds, which must be buried one year before they grow, in a dry rich upland soil. It may likewise grow by suckers and layers.

The timber is preferred by the turner to beech; he fashions it into cups, dishes, trays, tables, and the joiner into panel work, doors, musical instruments, &c. The grain in fineness of texture may almost compare with the cedar. Cicero paid for a table made of maple six hundred dollars; King Juba nine hundred; another in those days was valued at eight thousand four hundred dollars, and still another at its weight in gold. This last was four and a half feet in diameter, and three inches thick. For polishing this wood, a man's hand directly from the bath is better than any cloth.

Setting out the sap buckets near Groton, Vermont. (Photo courtesy of Dick Smith.)

The undulations of the curled or bird's-eye maple is probably caused by the ascent and descent of sap, being diverted by the numerous branches projecting from the trunk: There are nine varieties, viz: the mountain maple (acer montanum), box elder (acer negundo), sugar maple (acer saccharinum), black sugar maple (acer nigrum), Norway maple (acer platanoidea), sycamore (acer pseudo-platanus), moose wood (acer striatum), white maple (acer eriocarpum), red flowering maple (acer rubrum). . . .

General Chandler.—For the last twenty-five years maple sugar in various degrees of refinement has been exhibited at our fairs, some of it very highly refined. In its most unrefined state it has a flavor which tastes of the tree, is peculiarly agreeable; but in proportion as it is refined, it more and more resembles that of the sugar cane.

Chairman.—To retard the souring of fresh sap they use a very small quantity of sulphate of lime. The acidity begins almost immediately after the sap is drawn from the tree.

The Farmers Club report probably included my father's grandmother among the Ohio producers. She wrote in her diary in 1845: "We have taken a lease for eight years on a lot of forty acres on which there is an old clearing of 10 or 12 acres. We are bound to reclear the old, and ten acres more in the green, build a cabin, dig and wall a well, plant out 30 fruit trees, and if we make sugar on the lot we must give every fifth pound." She had come down from Vermont in 1818, her family lured there by stories of the easy living in the Ohio Country, and undoubtedly supervised the sugar making on this tract just north of the Wyandotte Reservation near Upper Sandusky.

The year 1852 was probably the top year for maple syrup and sugar production in this country, and production dropped off precipitously to almost zero by the late 1960s.

The causes of the decline were competition from cane and beet sugar and a universal restlessness and movement throughout the country. Improved transportation had made cane sugar and molasses from the South available to all but the most isolated communities. The Chinese indentured servants brought to Hawaii in 1852 helped the flow of cane sugar pro-

duced by the slaves elsewhere. Napoleon I had popularized beet sugar in areas where cane would not grow, and in 1852 Brigham Young ordered sugar refining equipment from Europe for his colony in Utah.

The year 1852 brought the publication of Harriet Beecher Stowe's *Uncle Tom's Cabin,* and within nine years the young men of the country had left their farms, and their maples, to engage in the bloody battles of the Civil War. That same year also marked the height of the rush to the gold fields of California and Nevada, and the beginning of the general awareness of the vast, unoccupied, unsettled farm lands west of the Mississippi.

Like thousands of mothers after the Civil War, great-grandmother Thompson joined her sons in the general exodus to the western prairies. Maple syrup making became a forgotten art. Vermont, forsaken once already, was again left to the women and old men, and to decay.

But if you are thinking of acquiring a bit of cheap land in the country now, Vermont may not be for you. The grandsons have come home from California and the Klondike, and the city folks have already swarmed up there to enjoy the beauty, quiet, and clean air and water. Many of them want to be a part of the land, partners with the land, to do their own living and their own creating without being answerable to a supervisor or a machine.

Agricultural economics as we know it today precludes entering farming as a career to all but the handful who may acquire the agribusiness by inheritance. To keep the agribusiness from insolvency they are taught to commit—*forced* to commit—flagrant violations of the concept of stewardship. In the late 1930s in Iowa's largest farm land foreclosure case, Equitable Life Assurance Society *vs.* Collins, Equitable was allowed to effect a foreclosure because Collins had committed "waste." He had pulled out groves and fence lines, consolidated farms and torn down the buildings. His tractors compacted the soil and he raised no livestock. Now all of these new agribusinessmen, so-called farmers, are doing the same thing, plus engaging in a host of other practices which might be construed as "waste" and which are certainly not considered stewardship.

There is room in the outlying country, however, for men and women of good will, intelligence and determination. Full-time subsistence farming can be most difficult and discouraging, but a compromise permitting even some country living is worth the effort. There may be little room left in Vermont, but do check the maple maps in Chapter 2 now. You probably have an opportunity waiting at your doorstep. Our ancestors were maple sugar makers, and surely we can do as well as they did.

NOTE: The substantial credit given to the Indians by historians for introducing maple sugar or syrup to the early American colonists seems unwarranted. The northern Indians who did make sugar were few in number. They were primarily hunters, and there is little to indicate that they had pots substantial enough to evaporate more than a minuscule amount of sap. Heated stones, reportedly, were dropped into the pots—but if you have ever tried this method you will realize its limited usefulness in heating water or evaporating sap.

The iron, copper and brass kettles made by the early explorers and colonists were traded for furs, corn and the like, and were, in fact, as important to the westward expansion as the gun and the ax and the hoe.

NOTE: Today's "back-to-the-land" people might be interested in the diets of the coastal Indians, as described by Dr. Bennett. He states that the coastal Indians never faced the chronic starvation most less-settled tribes did. They relied primarily upon corn, using 1,344 pounds per year for a family of five, which gave each member roughly 1,150 calories or 65% of their total daily caloric intake. Animal and bird carcasses supplied 10%

more, fish 9%, nuts and leguminous seeds 8%, eggs 1%, grain alternatives such as groundnuts, *Apios tuberosa,* and Jerusalem artichokes 2%, such vegetables and fruits as beans, squash, berries and pumpkins 4%, and visible vegetable fats such as oil from the walnut and white-oak acorns the remaining 1%.

Scurvy does not seem to have been prevalent, Dr. Bennett believes, "but to attempt to appraise the nutritional adequacy of the Indian diet with respect either to ascorbic acid or any other vitamin or mineral would seem to be merely an exercise in conjecture. . . . Corn, beans, squashes, pumpkins, and the nonfood tobacco were the standard items cultivated."

In any event, as Dr. Bennett quotes from Josselyn, "The Indesses that are young, are . . . generally plump of their Bodies, as are the men likewise, and as soft and smooth as the mole-skin. . . . The . . . old women are lean and uglie."

Nothing, absolutely nothing, is as soft and smooth as a mole's skin! Each one is about two inches square. Obtaining enough skins to make a coat, as I once considered doing for my mother, is virtually impossible.

10

Recipes

We may live without poetry, music and art;
We may live without conscience and live without heart;
We may live without friends, we may live without books;
But civilized men cannot live without cooks.

—Owen Meredith

Maple syrup is a delicious, versatile ingredient in baking or cooking—try it in some of your own favorite recipes. It may be added to salad dressings or used in simple fruit desserts to serve as the flavoring and sweetening agent. Bread, cakes and cookies can also be flavored with maple syrup. Always begin with a basic recipe, and then develop ideas for maple syrup in your meals.

One tablespoon of pure maple syrup contains 50 calories, and gives 5% of the recommended daily iron allowance. While maple syrup and maple sugar are similar to other natural sweeteners in nutritional value, their delicate flavors make them a premium food. This unrefined, pure product is favored by a growing number of concerned mothers.

Grandma Thompson raised a bunch of husky children—my father lived to be 95—and she swore by natural maple sugar. We would like to share some of our favorite recipes from her *Kitchen Journal* with you. A few of them are from my daughter, a true gourmet cook who is partial to braided rugs and homespun, wholesome things.

Use maple syrup:
> On griddlecakes or french toast
> > warm biscuits or steamed rice
> > ice cream or apple pie
> > corn fritters or cooked cereals
> > grapefruit
>
> To make a delicious maple milk shake or eggnog

Use granulated maple sugar:
> On baked apples
> > cooked cereal
>
> To sprinkle on hot buttered toast
> > sprinkle over ice cream
>
> In baking

Keep maple syrup refrigerated after opening.

Basic information

In the following recipes note the differences in temperature. As maple syrup becomes more concentrated, its temperature will rise; the final results are basically related to the initial syrup concentration. But don't be too concerned about absolute accuracy in temperature and timing: no matter when you take the syrup off the stove, you'll have something nice.

When a small quantity of syrup cooked to the following temperatures is dropped into ice water it will form:

> Thread—230–234°
> Soft ball—234–240°
> Firm ball—244–248°
> Hard ball—250–256°
> Soft crack—270–290°
> Hard crack—300–310°
> Caramelized sugar—310–338°
> It will turn black at 350°.

```
PUBLIC SUGAR SUPPER
G.A.R. Memorial Hall
Saturday, March 19, 1939
Served from 5 p.m.
Auspices Daughter of Union Veterans
Menu: Baked Beans, Cottage Cheese,
Rolls, Pickles, Doughnuts, Sugar on
Snow, Coffee.
PRICE—30 Cents
```

Newspaper notices like the one above attested to the continuing popularity of old-fashioned Sugar Suppers held at sugaring time. This recipe was developed from the method of testing the thickness of syrup when maple sap was boiled down in the woods. Sugar on snow with unsweetened doughnuts, pickles and coffee are the basis of the famous Vermont Sugar Suppers.

Maple Sugar on Snow

Prepare a pan of fresh, clean snow. Boil maple syrup until a spoonful, dropped on the snow, does not sink in and vanish but forms a waxy candy on top. Serve hot in cups, offering with each cup a pan of fresh snow. The hot syrup is trickled over the snow and the waxy candy thus formed is rolled up on a fork and eaten at once.

Basic syrups and sugars

To Make Maple Syrup

To convert maple sugar into syrup, add 1 part of water to 2 parts of sugar by weight and boil until dissolved and clear. If you have a thermometer it should be about 219°F. You now have a maple syrup very delicious on hot biscuits, cakes or waffles.

To Make Maple Sugar

If you want to make maple sugar, take syrup and boil until it forms a soft ball, at 240°F. Whip until almost cool and pour in mold. This is a regular form of maple sugar.

Hot Spiced Maple-Honey Syrup

A Colonial recipe to be used on pancakes, waffles, puddings or what you will. It is deliciously different.

1 c maple syrup	½ t cinnamon (powered)
½ c strained honey	½ t caraway seeds

In a saucepan, mix the maple syrup with the honey. Add cinnamon and caraway seeds. Set over a flame and allow to come to a hard boil. Remove from stove, pour into a sauceboat, pottery pitcher or syrup jug, and carry to the table. When this is to be used with pancakes or waffles, serve it with a pitcher of hot melted butter. Use the butter first and then top with the Spiced Maple-Honey Syrup.

Breads, fritters, muffins and rolls

Maple Syrup Brown Bread

(Makes 2 loaves)

¾ c uncooked rolled oats	¼ c butter or margarine
1¼ c boiling water	2 t salt
1 package active dry yeast	5 c all-purpose flour
	1 c whole wheat flour
¼ c warm water (105° to 115°)	½ c golden raisins
	Pure maple or maple-blended syrup, if
½ c milk	desired
⅓ c pure maple or maple-blended syrup	Maple or dark-brown sugar, if desired
¼ c granulated sugar	

Combine oats and 1¼ cups water in small bowl. Cover. Let stand until water is absorbed, about 20 minutes.

Meanwhile, dissolve yeast in warm water in large bowl. Let stand until bubbly, about 5 minutes. Combine milk, ⅓ cup syrup, the granulated sugar, butter and salt in small saucepan. Heat over low heat until butter is melted. Cool to lukewarm. Stir into yeast; add oats mixture. Mix in flour and raisins to make stiff dough. Turn dough onto lightly floured surface. Knead until smooth and elastic, about 10 minutes. Place in greased bowl; turn greased side up and cover with towel. Let rise in warm place until double, about 1½ hours. (Dough is ready if impression remains.)

Punch down dough; divide in half. Roll each half into rectangle, 16×8". Roll up, beginning at short edge. Pinch ends together to seal. Place seam side down in 2 greased loaf pans, 8½×4½×2½". Cover; let rise until double, about 1½ hours.

Heat oven to 375°F. Bake 40 to 45 minutes. Cool in pans 10 minutes; remove from pans. Brush tops with maple syrup and sprinkle with maple sugar while still warm. Cool on wire rack.

Maple Fritters

3 eggs, well-beaten	2 c milk
1 t cream	2 t baking powder
½ t salt	4 c flour

Mix the baking powder thoroughly with the flour, add the flour to the milk, add the salt, then the eggs. Fry in hot shortening. Serve hot, with warm maple syrup.

Maple Sugar Biscuits

2 c sifted flour	4 t butter or other
3 t baking powder	shortening
½ t salt	¾ c milk

Sift dry ingredients together. Add the butter or other shortening, working it in with a fork or dough blender. Add milk to make a soft dough. Place on a floured board and toss lightly until the outer surface looks smooth. Roll out ½" thick and cut with floured biscuit cutter. Place on a greased pan and bake in a very hot oven, 450°F for about 12 minutes. Makes 14 2-inch biscuits.

Variations: Before baking, brush tops of biscuits with butter and sprinkle generously with grated maple sugar. Or fold ½ c crushed maple sugar into biscuit dough before rolling and cutting.

Maple Brown-'N-Serve Rolls

¼ c butter	½ t grated orange
⅓ c honey	¼ t salt
1 c maple syrup	⅓ c chopped pecans

Melt butter in quart saucepan. Stir in maple syrup, honey, grated orange rind and salt. Boil over medium heat 12 minutes, stirring. Remove from heat; stir in pecans. Spoon 2 T of mixture into each muffin pan cup. Place rolls top side down in each muffin cup. Butter bottom of each roll. Bake in preheated oven 375°F for 10 minutes. Turn over on serving place and serve with butter.

Maple Date-Nut Bread

(Makes 1 loaf)

1 c boiling water	1 c cake flour, sifted
1 c chopped dates	1 t baking powder
1 T butter	1 t salt
1 egg, beaten	¾ t soda
½ c maple syrup	1 c whole wheat flour
½ c chopped pecans	

Pour boiling water over dates and butter. Stir until butter melts. Add beaten egg, maple syrup and chopped nuts. Sift together the flour, baking powder, salt and soda. Combine with the whole wheat flour. Pour the liquid mixture into the dry ingredients. Stir until just dampened. Pour into a greased loaf pan and bake at 350°F for 1 hour. Let cool thoroughly before slicing.

Maple All-Bran Muffins

Moisten 1 c bran cereal with ¾ c milk. Add 2 T melted shortening, 1 well-beaten egg and ⅓ c dark maple syrup.

Sift together 1 c flour, 3 t baking powder and 1 t salt.

Combine ingredients. Stir only enough to moisten. Fill greased muffin tins ⅔ full. Bake in 400–425°F oven for 15 minutes.

Maple Fritters

4 c sifted flour	1 t sweet cream
2 t baking powder	3 eggs, well beaten
½ t salt	confectioners' sugar
2 c sweet milk	

Sift dry ingredients together and add to milk and cream. Slowly add well-beaten eggs, stirring constantly. Drop by spoonfuls into hot deep fat (360°F) and fry until well-puffed and browned. Sprinkle with confectioners' sugar and serve hot with warm maple syrup pudding sauce. Serves 12.

Maple Rolls

2½	c sifted flour	1	c finely chopped
3	t baking powder		apples
½	t salt	½	c raisins
4	T butter or other	½	c sugar
	shortening	1	t cinnamon
¾	c milk	½	c maple sugar
¾	c water		

Sift flour, baking powder and salt together. Cut 3 T butter or other shortening into dry ingredients and add milk slowly, mixing to make a smooth dough. Roll about ¼″ thick on a floured board and spread with apples, raisins, sugar and cinnamon which have been mixed together. (Strawberry or raspberry jam may be used instead of apple mixture.) Roll like a jelly roll and cut across in 2-inch slices. Place the slices in a well-greased baking pan with the cut side down. Sprinkle well with the maple sugar, dot with remaining butter and add water. Bake in a hot oven (400°F) about 30 minutes, basting often with the sauce in the pan. Serve with a sauce made from sweet cream, a little maple sugar and a dash of grated nutmeg, or with maple syrup pudding sauce. Serves 8.

Cakes

Maple Angel Cake

¼	c cake flour	1¼	c egg whites
1½	c maple syrup	1	t cream of tartar
½	t salt		

Sift flour several times before measuring. Boil maple syrup until it spins a thread. Add salt to egg whites and beat till foamy. Add cream of tarter and beat until stiff, but not dry. Pour hot syrup in fine stream on egg whites while beating constantly and continue beating until mixture is cool. Fold in flour a small amount at a time. Bake 1 hour at 325°F.

Maple Gingerbread Cake

(Makes 13×9" cake)

½ c butter or margarine	3 c all-purpose flour
2 eggs	2 t baking soda
1½ c pure maple or maple-blended syrup	1½ t ground ginger
	½ t salt
	Chopped walnuts
1½ c dairy sour cream	

Cream butter in large mixer bowl until light and fluffy. Beat in eggs, syrup and sour cream. Beat in flour, soda, ginger and salt. Pour batter into greased and floured baking pan, 13×9×2". Bake until wooden pick inserted in center comes out clean, about 40 minutes. Cool in pan on wire rack.

Make maple frosting; spread maple frosting on cake and sprinkle with chopped walnuts.

Maple Syrup Gingerbread

1 c maple syrup	1 t baking soda
1 c sour cream	1½ t ginger
1 egg, well beaten	½ t salt
2⅓ c sifted flour	4 T melted butter

Blend maple syrup, sour cream and egg together. Sift dry ingredients and stir into liquid, beating well. Add butter or other shortening and beat thoroughly. Pour into an oblong baking pan, which has been lined with waxed paper, and bake at 350° for 30 minutes. Serves 8 to 10.

Maple Syrup Cake I

½ c sugar	Pinch of salt
⅓ c shortening	2¼ c flour
¾ c maple syrup	3 T baking powder
½ c milk	3 egg whites

Cream shortening. Gradually add half the sugar; cream until fluffy. Beat in the syrup. Stir in sifted dry ingredients (except sugar) alternately with milk. Beat egg whites until soft peaks form; gradually add rest of sugar and beat until peaks round over gently. Fold into batter. Bake in 13×9½×2″ pan at 350°F for 45–60 minutes. Cool; frost with maple sugar frosting.

Maple Syrup Cake II

2	c shortening	½	t soda
½	c granulated sugar	2	t baking powder
1	whole egg	½	t ginger
1	egg yolk	½	c hot water
1	c maple syrup	½	t salt
2½	c cake flour		

Cream shortening and sugar. Add whole egg and egg yolk, beaten together. Sift and measure flour, then sift again with ginger, soda, baking powder and salt. Add to first mixture alternately with the water. Bake in a tube tin at 375°F about 50 minutes. Cover with maple icing and decorate with walnuts.

Maple Nut Cake

1	c maple sugar	2	eggs, well-beaten
2	c flour	1	c chopped English
1	c chopped raisins		walnuts
3	t baking powder	½	c butter
½	c sweet milk		

Beat the butter to a cream. Add the sugar gradually. When light add the eggs, then the milk, and last the flour in which the baking powder has been thoroughly mixed. Mix this quickly and add the nuts and raisins. Bake in a deep baking pan at 350°F for about 35 minutes. Finish cake with a cream frosting.

Maple Loaf Cake with Maple Foam Icing

⅓ c butter or margarine
½ c white sugar
1 t vanilla
1½ t baking powder
¼ c maple syrup
1½ c flour (sifted once
    before measuring
    and twice afterward)

½ c milk
1 egg, separated
Pinch of salt

Cream butter and sugar. Add well-beaten egg yolk, then vanilla and syrup. Add flour, alternating with the milk. Add baking powder and, last of all, fold in the egg white, stiffly beaten with a few grains of salt. Pour into a buttered loaf pan (about 5×9″) and bake in a moderate oven (375°F) for from 45 minutes to 1 hour, or until cake tests done. Let it stand a few moments before removing from the pan. Stand on a wire cake rack or towel placed over a board until cake is cool.

Maple Upside-Down Cake

3 T butter
1 c maple sugar
4 slices pineapple
3 eggs, separated and
    beaten
1 c granulated sugar

½ c water
½ t vanilla
½ t lemon extract
1 c sifted flour
1½ t baking powder

Melt butter, without browning, in a heavy skillet. Remove from heat, spread maple sugar over bottom of skillet and cover with a layer of sliced pineapple. To beaten egg yolks add granulated sugar, water, vanilla and lemon extract; beat until thick and lemon-colored. Add dry ingredients, sifted together, and beat for 3 minutes. Fold in beaten egg whites. Pour over pineapple in skillet and bake in a moderate oven (350°F) for about 45 minutes. Loosen cake from sides and bottom and turn out on cake rack immediately. Serves 8.

Candy

Making Taffy Candy

For the following two maple taffy recipes, follow these general directions for cooking and pulling.

When candy reaches 270°, pour onto a buttered plate, being careful not to splash it. Use a candy scraper to work the taffy into a central mass. With buttered fingers, pull and twist the taffy to about 18″ for about 5 minutes. Form a 1″-thick rope and cut with buttered shears onto a board dusted with powdered sugar or cornstarch.

To Make Maple Taffy, or *Spotza*

Boil maple syrup to 258°F. Swirl a spoonful on packed snow or finely cracked ice and pick up by twisting on a wooden fork or spoon or with the fingers. This is a tasty taffy for use at *Spotza* parties. *Spotza* is a Pennsylvania Dutch name for taffy. The hot liquid may be poured into an aluminum foil pan or buttered dish, wrapped tightly, and stored in a freezer. It is then brittle enough to be cracked with a hammer or heavy spoon for eating.

Maple Candy

     2 c maple sugar
    ½ c of water
     1 T vinegar

Boil mixture until it is crumbly when dropped into cold water. Turn onto buttered plates; when cool enough, pull and cut into sticks.

Maple Cream

2 c maple sugar
½ c cream
1 c nuts (preferably
   butternuts)

Boil sugar and cream until mixture spins a thread, then stir in nuts. Pour into buttered tins and when nearly cold cut into squares.

Maple Cream Candy I

Boil maple syrup briskly to 234°F, or to soft ball stage. Keep sides of pan free from crystals. Pour syrup about ¾″ deep in shallow dish. Do not scrape pan when pouring syrup. Cool to lukewarm. When cool, stir with spoon until light and creamy. Pour into greased dish. Mark in squares.

Maple Cream Candy II

2 c maple syrup
1 t vanilla

Boil syrup over very low heat, without stirring, until it reaches the late thread stage (about 233°). Allow the reduced syrup to cool to 110° without stirring— about 1 hour. Add vanilla. Beat until the mixture is light and fluffy, and firm enough to hold its shape as patties or in molds. Put candy in a tightly covered container as soon as it cools to keep it from drying out.

Maple Divinity

2 c maple syrup   ⅓ c chopped pecans
¼ t salt
2 egg whites, beaten
    stiff

Boil maple syrup to 250°F without stirring. Add salt and pour mixture slowly over egg whites. Beat the whole mixture until it holds its shape. Add the nuts and drop by spoonsful onto wax paper.

Maple Divinity Fudge

2 c sugar   2 egg whites
½ c corn syrup   ¾ c blanched almonds
½ c maple syrup   1 T almond or lemon
½ water   extract
¾ c candied cherries

Put the sugar, water, maple and corn syrup into a saucepan. Stir it while it dissolves over the fire, then let it boil without stirring to the light crack stage (265°F). While it is cooking, beat the egg whites until stiff and when the syrup is ready pour it over them, beating constantly. Beat until creamy. Add nuts, cherries and extract and pour into buttered tins.

Maple Fudge

1 c granulated sugar   ½ c milk or cream
2 c maple syrup   1 T butter
¼ c white Karo   1 T flour

Combine all ingredients except butter. Cook to 232°F. Add butter; cool and beat. Pour into greased cake pan. When cool, cut into squares.

Maple Nut Brittle

1 c light brown sugar	1 t vanilla
1 c maple sugar	¼ t salt
½ c water	1 c broken nut meats
2 T butter	

Boil the sugar and water to the stiff-ball stage (246°F). Add butter and cook to the brittle stage (290–300°F). Add the vanilla and salt and pour over the nut meats, which have been placed on a buttered pan. When cold, break into pieces.

Maple Nut Candy

1 T vinegar	2 pounds sugar
Butter	Maple sugar
Nuts, chopped	

Use maple sugar with sufficient water to dissolve it, 1 T vinegar to 2 pounds of sugar, and butter the size of a walnut. Boil to 260°F, or hard-ball stage. Pour immediately into buttered pan in which chopped nuts have been placed. Mark in strips before cold.

Maple Pralines I

2 c sugar	2 c nutmeats, preferably
3 c milk	pecan
1 c maple syrup	

Boil the sugar, milk and maple syrup until the mixture reaches the soft-ball stage (238°F). Remove from the fire and cool. When lukewarm, beat until smooth and creamy. Add any kind of broken nutmeats and drop onto buttered paper from the tip of a spoon, making little mounds.

Maple Pralines II

1⅞ c powdered sugar   2 c nutmeats (broken
2 c cream   hickory or black
1 c maple sugar   walnuts)

Put sugars and cream into suacepan and boil to soft-ball stage
(234°F). Let stand until cool. Beat with a wooden spoon until
thick. Add nuts, then drop from tip of spoon onto wax paper
or spread in a buttered pan about 9×9″ and cut into squares.
Makes 1½ pounds.

Maple Puffs

2 c maple syrup   Pinch of salt
1 c water   2 c nutmeats, preferably
4 egg whites   walnut
2 pounds maple sugar

Cook maple syrup, sugar and water with salt to 260°F. Remove
from the fire and let stand for 3 or 4 minutes. Slowly pour the
sugar mixture into the well-beaten egg whites. When thick, stir
in 2 c walnut meats and drop by spoonfuls onto heavily waxed
paper. Work quickly so that all can be finished before the batch
hardens.

Maple Scotch

1 c maple sugar   1 t vinegar
½ c water   4 T butter

Boil the maple sugar, water and vinegar together to the hard
ball stage (246°F). Add the butter and cook to the medium-
crack stage (280°F). Turn into a well-buttered pan. Mark while
still warm, and when cold break into pieces.

Maple Popped Corn
and Nut Candy

1 T butter
1 c maple sugar

3 quarts popped corn
3 T water

Boil butter, water and maple sugar until mixture is ready to candy and then add three quarts of nicely popped corn. Stir briskly until mixture is evenly distributed over the corn. Keep stirring until mixture cools and each kernel is separately coated. Close and undivided attention is necessary for the success of this kind of candy. Nuts are also delicious prepared by this method.

Maple Nut Creams

3 c maple sugar
1 c cream or evaporated
  milk
2 c butternuts, walnuts
  or pecans

2 t maple flavoring
1 T butter

Stir sugar and cream together until sugar dissolves. Boil to 234°F or until a little of the mixture forms a soft ball when dropped into cold water. Cool to lukewarm. Add maple flavoring, butter and nuts and beat until creamy. Drop from spoon onto waxed paper. Makes 3 dozen candies.

Maple Caramels

2 c brown sugar
1½ c maple syrup

½ c cream
1 T butter

Stir sugar, syrup and cream in a large, heavy pan over quick heat until sugar is dissolved. Still stirring, cook these ingredients slowly to the firm ball stage (242°). Add butter. Pour candy onto buttered tin and cut into squares as it hardens.

Variations: Nuts may be added to the candy just before removing it from the heat, or they may be sprinkled on the buttered tin before pouring the candy. When cool, after about 3 hours, invert the candy onto a board and cut into squares.

Cookies

Coconut Maple Bars

1¼	c all-purpose flour	4	t salt
¼	c sugar	1	c shredded coconut
⅔	c butter or margarine	½	t vanilla
⅔	c maple syrup		

Mix flour, sugar and ½ c butter and crumble mixture into coarse crumbs. Press firmly into bottom of 9×9″-square pan. Bake at medium heat for 12–50 minutes or until lightly browned. Mix syrup, remaining butter and salt together. Cook, stirring occasionally, until slightly thickened. Remove from heat; add coconut and vanilla. Spread over crumb mixture; return to oven. Bake 15 minutes longer or until top is browned. Cut into squares while warm.

Maple Sugar Cookies I

½	c butter or other shortening	½	t lemon extract
		1	T milk
1	c maple sugar, rolled and sifted	2½	c sifted cake flour
		1	t salt
2	eggs, beaten	2½	t baking powder

Sift part of the flour with salt and baking powder. Cream shortening, add the maple sugar and cream well again. Add eggs, lemon extract, milk and the sifted flour mixture. Beat well and add remaining flour. Chill dough about ½ hour in refrigerator. Roll ¼ inch thick, sprinkle with brown sugar and cut into attractive shapes with cookie cutters. Place on a greased cookie sheet and bake in a moderate oven (350°F) about 15 minutes. Makes about 3 dozen cookies.

Maple Sugar Cookies II

2¼ c sifted flour	1 c maple sugar, sifted
¼ t salt	2 eggs, beaten
2 t baking powder	½ t vanilla
½ c shortening	1 T milk

Sift flour, salt and baking powder together. Cream shortening and sugar together, add eggs and vanilla, and mix well. Add sifted ingredients and milk. Roll and cut with a cookie cutter or the rim of a glass dipped in sugar. Sprinkle with sugar and bake on baking sheet in moderate oven (375°F) 12 minutes. Makes 2½ dozen cookies.

Maple Sugar Cookies III

2 c maple syrup	4 eggs, well-beaten
Flour (about 5 cups)	1 c milk
1 c butter	2 t baking powder

Beat the sugar and the butter to a cream. Add the eggs and next add the flour in which the baking powder has been well-mixed. Use just enough flour to make dough easy to roll. Roll dough and cut into any form to suit the taste. Bake in 350°F oven.

Maple Hermit Bars

½	c butter	¾	c maple sugar
¼	t cloves	1	t cinnamon
½	t soda	1	T milk
1	egg, beaten	2½	c flour
½	t soda	½	c currants

Cream butter; gradually beat in sugar, cloves and cinnamon. Dissolve soda in milk and beat this into sugar and butter. Add beaten egg. Add flour, soda and currants. Roll out an inch thick on a floured board and cut into squares. Bake on a cookie sheet in hot oven (425°F) 12 minutes.

Maple Nut Brownies

¼	c shortening	2	squares chocolate
½	c maple syrup	1	t vanilla
½	c sugar	2	eggs, beaten
½	c sifted flour	¼	t baking powder
¼	t salt	1	c chopped nuts

Melt shortening and chocolate together; add maple syrup, vanilla, sugar and eggs. Sift flour, baking powder and salt, and then add nuts. Add this to first mixture. Bake in a shallow pan, which has been lined with well-greased waxed paper, in a slow oven (300°F) for 45 minutes.

Maple Nut Cookies

1½ c maple sugar
1 c butter
3 eggs
3 c flour
1 t baking soda,
   dissolved in ½ c hot
   water

1½ c date pieces
1 t baking powder

Mix all the above ingredients together in a large bowl. Drop from a teaspoon onto a baking sheet and bake in a moderate oven (350°F) until firm. Store in a metal container or cookie jar —maple nut cookies improve with age.

Maple Ginger Snaps

2 c maple sugar
1 t baking soda
1 c butter
2 T ginger

1 c sour cream
Flour (enough to make
   a stiff paste)
2 eggs

Mix ingredients. Roll dough thin, cut and bake at 375°F until done.

Old-Fashioned Maple Sugar Drop Cookies

½ c butter
1 egg or 2 egg yolks
1 T cream or milk
¼ t salt

¾ c maple sugar
½ t vanilla
1¼ c flour
¼ t baking powder

Cream butter until light and fluffy. Beat in maple sugar; add eggs and vanilla. Beat thoroughly and add cream. Sift dry ingredients, add to butter mixture. Mix well and arrange by teaspoonful on a buttered cookie sheet, 1 inch apart. Bake about 8 minutes at 375°F. Makes 50 to 60 cookies.

Custards

Maple Charlotte Russe

1 envelope (1 T)
  unflavored
  granulated gelatin
½ c cold water
½ c scalded milk
¼ c brown sugar

½ c maple syrup
1 t vanilla
1 pint heavy cream,
  whipped
Lady fingers

Cook gelatin and water over low heat until gelatin dissolves. Add milk, brown sugar, maple syrup and vanilla. Chill until almost firm. Beat until fluffy. Beat half of the whipped cream into the mixture; fold in the rest. Line a number of small molds, or one large deep mold, with a thick layer of cake. Thin sponge cake that has been cut when cold with a sharp knife into two equal layers is attractive, but halved lady fingers or pieces of plain cake cut ½-inch thick may be used. Fill the forms. Keep the charlottes on ice until needed, and serve on chilled plates.

Maple Custard

4 egg yolks
¾ c maple syrup
4 c milk
¾ c chopped nutmeats
  (butternut are
  excellent)

4 egg whites
⅛ t salt

Beat yolks and syrup together. Add milk and nutmeats. Whip egg whites with salt until stiff. Fold the custard into the egg whites. Fill individual custard cups with the mixture. Place them in a pan of hot water and bake at 325°F until custard is firm. Serves 4–6.

Frozen Maple Custard

1 c maple syrup
1 c milk
1 c cream, whipped until stiff

4 eggs, separated and beaten
2 T flour

Add beaten yolks to syrup and cook over hot water, stirring constantly until mixture boils. Add milk and flour stirred to a smooth paste. Bring again to boiling point, then remove from the fire. When cold, fold in whipped cream. Turn into trays and partially freeze. Then add stiffly beaten whites of eggs and return to freezer. Can be served in two hours.

Quick Charlotte

1 c maple syrup
1 envelope gelatin (1 T)
1 pint heavy cream, whipped

Lady fingers

Cook syrup and gelatin over moderate heat until the gelatin dissolves, stirring constantly. Chill until slightly thick. Fold in cream. Line a mold or paper cups with lady fingers; fill with charlotte and chill. Serves 6–8.

Dressings

Maple Fruit Salad Dressing

1 c malt vinegar	Juice and pulp of
3 t salt	small onion, grated
¼ t paprika	(about 1 T)
Dash of tabasco, or	½ to ¾ c maple syrup
more if you prefer	1 c olive oil or ½ c oil
hot dressing	and ½ c salad oil

Place the malt vinegar in a mixing bowl and add salt, paprika, tabasco, onion juice and pulp. Mix well. Add maple syrup. Stir until blended, then add olive oil. Pour into a bottle or jar and shake well. This dressing is especially good with pear or pineapple or any fruit salad, cheese and fruit aspics, or any salad requiring a sweet dressing.

Variations: Add ¼ t poultry seasoning and ¼ t dry mustard to above dressing, mixing these ingredients with the vinegar and proceeding as above. This gives a much spicier flavor.

Maple Salad Dressing

1 T flour	1 c cream, whipped
¼ c lemon juice	½ t salt
½ c maple syrup	Speck of pepper

Mix flour with lemon juice until lumps are gone. Add to syrup and cook while stirring until mixture is thick as honey. Cool. Fold whipped cream into the cold mixture. Add salt and pepper. Serve on fruit salad.

Dumplings

Maple Apple Dumplings

Dumpling Pastry
(recipe follows)
6 T mincemeat
6 T shredded Cheddar
cheese
1 egg yolk
6 small Golden
Delicious or
Cortland apples,
pared and cored

3 T maple or dark brown
sugar
3 T milk

Make Dumpling Pastry. Fill each apple with 1 T mincemeat, 1 T cheese and ½ T maple sugar. Fold Dumpling Pastry circles over apples, joining pastry at blossom end of apple; moisten and seal edges of pastry. Place in buttered baking cups, seam side down. Mix egg yolk and milk in small bowl; brush surface of pastries with egg yolk mixture. Bake at 425°F until golden, about 40 minutes. Serves 6.

Maple Dumpling Pastry

2½ c all-purpose flour
1 t salt

¾ c shortening
5–6 T cold water

Mix flour and salt in medium-size bowl. Cut in lard until mixture resembles coarse crumbs. Sprinkle with water, 1 T at a time, mixing until flour is moistened and dough cleans side of bowl. Gather dough into ball and divide into sixths. Shape into six flattened rounds on lightly-floured surface. Roll each round of dough ¼-inch thick. Trim to 8-inch circle.

Frostings & fillings

Boiled Maple Icing

1 c maple syrup	½ c cold water
⅛ t cream of tartar	2 egg whites, beaten
1 t vanilla	

Combine sugar, cream of tartar and water and boil to 238°F, or until a little of the syrup forms a soft ball when dropped into cold water. Pour hot syrup very slowly into the beaten egg whites, beating constantly. Flavor with vanilla and beat until icing is cool and of proper consistency to spread. Frosts tops and sides of two 9-inch layers.

Boiled Maple Frosting
(use on German chocolate cake)

4 egg yolks, beaten	½ c butter
1 c evaporated milk	½ c coconut
1 c maple sugar	½ c nutmeats, chopped

Combine ingredients and cook over boiling water until it thickens (takes quite a while). When thick, take off stove and stir several minutes; cool. Add coconut and nutmeats. Frost center and top of cake.

Maple Frosting

3 T pure maple or maple-blended syrup	2 T butter or margarine
	1 T dairy sour cream
	2½ c powdered sugar

Beat syrup, butter and sour cream in small mixer bowl on low speed until creamy. Beat in powdered sugar gradually, scraping bowl occasionally. Beat frosting until smooth.

Maple Fudge Frosting

1⅓	c sugar	½	c butter
⅔	c grated maple sugar	⅔	c cream

Mix all ingredients in saucepan; cook about 13 minutes to the soft-ball stage (234°F). Cool. Beat until thick enough to spread.

Quick Maple Icing

2	c confectioners' sugar, sifted	¼	t salt
		½	t vanilla
1	T butter		Maple Syrup

Sift confectioners' sugar. Blend in butter, salt and vanilla. Beat in enough maple syrup to make icing a good consistency for spreading.

Variations: ½ c toasted coconut may be added.

Maple Icing

¾	c maple syrup	1	egg white, beaten
¼	c granulated sugar	⅛	t salt
¼	c water		

Boil sugar, maple syrup and water until it spins a thread. Pour over the beaten egg to which salt has been added. Beat until cool enough to spread.

Maple Marshmallow Frosting

1 c maple sugar	6 marshmallows or 2 T
½ c boiling water	marshmallow cream
2 egg whites	½ t vanilla

Cook the sugar and water together, stirring until the sugar is dissolved; then cook without stirring to the soft-ball stage (238°F). Add the marshmallow to the hot syrup, pressing it under the surface so that it will melt. (If individual marshmallows are used, cut them into small pieces.) Pour the syrup in a thin stream on to the stiffly beaten egg whites, beating the mixture constantly with a spoon. Add vanilla. Cool before spreading.

Maple Butter Frosting

½ c butter	¼ c chopped walnuts or
3 c confectioners' sugar	pecans
4–6 T maple syrup	

Thoroughly cream butter and sugar, adding maple syrup until light and spreadable. Add nuts and frost cake. Good on spice cake, applesauce cake or white cakes.

Maple Cream Filling

2 c maple syrup	1 T butter
¾ c milk	Pinch of salt

Cook syrup, milk, butter, and salt together to the soft-ball stage (238°F). Cool and beat until creamy. Use as a filling for cakes, creampuffs or tarts.

Maple Foam Icing

1 c maple or brown
   sugar
½ c maple syrup
Pinch of salt

2 T water
1 egg white
½ t vanilla

Boil sugar, syrup and water for 5 or 6 minutes until mixture is very thick and will spin a thread or make a hard ball in cold water. Meanwhile beat the egg white very stiff with a little salt. When the syrup is thick enough, pour a tablespoonful into the egg, beating vigorously all the while. *Two pairs of hands will be found helpful, as time is an important factor in making this icing.* Add another tablespoonful of syrup and another, until 4 T have been blended with the egg. Then quickly pour the rest of the syrup into the egg mixture, beating constantly. If an electric beater is handy, by all means use it. Add the vanilla and when icing is firm enough to stand in peaks, spread it over top and sides of cake. If beaten too long it is apt to become granular, and if not beaten enough it will not harden. Practice alone will tell when the moment is right for spreading this icing on the cake. However, it is delicious whether hard or soft or medium.

Maple Sauce

1 c maple syrup
3 egg whites

Cook syrup until it forms a soft ball in water. Beat whites of eggs until stiff and gradually beat in syrup. Beat until cool and serve as a sauce over warm cakes.

Seven-Minute Maple Frosting

½ c maple syrup
1 c sugar

¼ t cream of tartar
2 unbeaten egg whites

Put maple syrup, sugar, cream of tartar and egg whites into upper part of double boiler. Beat with rotary beater until thoroughly mixed. Place over rapidly boiling water. Beat constantly with beater and cook about 7 minutes or until frosting stands up in peaks. Remove from heat and beat until thick enough to spread.

Fruits

Baked Maple Apples I

4 tart apples
1 T cinnamon
¾ c boiling water

¼ c maple sugar
Butter
2 T sugar

Preheat oven to 375°F. Wash apples and remove core to within ½ inch of the stem end. Cut a strip of peel off around the top. Fill the hollowed apples with mixture of ¼ c maple sugar and cinnamon. Dot the tops with butter. Bake in a covered pan with ¾ c water and sugar for 40–60 minutes (baked apples should be tender but not mushy). Remove from oven and baste with juices. Serve warm or chilled—delicious with cream.

Baked Maple Apples II

Several tart apples
Maple sugar

Wash and core some good tart apples; set in baking dish and fill center of apples with maple sugar or syrup. Cover bottom of dish with ½ inch hot water. Bake in a moderate oven (350°F) until soft, basting occasionally with maple syrup.

Maple Apple Sauce

1 c maple sugar or
    syrup
	Unpeeled apple
	    sections

½ c water	

Bring maple sugar or syrup and water to rolling boil in a deep pan. Fill pan with unpeeled sections of apples. Stir up until all pieces are coated with syrup. Cook only long enough to tenderize apples. The slices remain unbroken and glazed.

Ice cream, parfait, mousse, milk shakes

Maple Ice Cream

1 quart cream	2 c maple syrup
2 eggs	1 pint milk
½ c flour, scant	

Bring milk to a boil. Beat 1 c syrup, flour and eggs until the mixture is light and creamy, then stir into the boiling milk; cook until the flour is thoroughly cooked. Set away to cool. When cold, whip the cream. Add whipped cream and second cup of syrup to cooked mixture and freeze in an ice cream freezer.

Refrigerator Maple Ice Cream

¼ c cold water	1 T gelatin

1 c hot milk or cream
    Pinch of salt
	⅜ c maple syrup or
	    maple sugar

1 egg yolk, slightly
    beaten
	1 pint heavy cream,
	    whipped

1 egg white, beaten stiff	1 t vanilla

Put water and gelatin in double boiler top, let stand 5 minutes, add hot milk and mix in syrup, flour and salt. Cook and stir over low heat until thick. Cover and cook over hot—but not boiling—water 10 minutes. Slowly stir in egg yolk; cook 1 minute. Strain into a refrigerator tray and put in the refrigerator until chilled. Spoon into a chilled bowl and beat with an egg beater until very light. Fold in cream, egg white, and vanilla. Pour back into the tray and freeze. Makes about 1 quart. If desired, add 1 c nutmeats, cut into pieces or chopped, stirring them into cream when nearly frozen.

Maple Parfait

¾ c maple syrup
3 egg whites
1 pint cream, stiffly
    whipped

Whipped cream for
topping

Cook maple syrup to the light-crack stage, 270°F. Pour the syrup over the beaten egg whites and beat until cold. Fold into the stiffly whipped cream. Mold and pack in ice and salt for 4 hours, or pack and freeze in the trays of the refrigerator. Serve in parfait glasses with whipped cream.

Maple Mousse I

2 T gelatin
¼ c cold water
1¼ c maple syrup

½ c sugar
5 c cream

Soften gelatin in water and dissolve over heat. Combine maple syrup, sugar and 1 c of cream and bring to a boil, stirring constantly. Add the gelatin. Strain, cool in ice water until the mixture thickens, then add the remainder of the cream, whipped stiff. Place in a mold, pack in ice and salt and let stand for 4 hours, or pack and freeze in the trays of the refrigerator.

Maple Mousse II

4 eggs or 6 egg yolks
1 pint heavy cream,
    whipped

⅔ c hot maple syrup
Pecan nut meats

Beat eggs slightly. Add the maple syrup little by little. Stir and cook in a double boiler until thick. Cool. Fold in cream. Freeze and then serve in parfait glasses. Sprinkle with nuts. Makes 1 quart or 8 small servings. Extravagant and high in calories, but a superb indulgence once in a while.

Maple Syrup Mousse

1 c maple syrup
3 eggs, separated
1 pint whipping cream

Whipped cream, if
   desired

Heat maple syrup in medium-size saucepan over medium heat to boiling; reduce heat. Boil over low heat, stirring constantly, 3 minutes. Remove from heat; cool 5 minutes. Beat egg yolks in small bowl until thick and lemon-colored. Stir ¼ c syrup gradually into eggs; beat 1 minute. Stir egg mixture into the remaining syrup. Cook and stir over low heat until thick, about 15 minutes. Cool 30 minutes. Beat egg whites until stiff but not dry; fold into cooled syrup mixture. Whip 1 pint whipping cream; fold into syrup mixture. Cover with aluminum foil; freeze at least 3 hours. Spoon into individual dessert bowls and garnish each serving with dollop of whipped cream. Makes 6 servings.

Super High-Protein Maple Shake

1 t powdered brewer's
   yeast
1 t maple syrup

1 c milk
2 T or more powdered
   skim milk

Blend ingredients together in an electric blender. You may flavor the milk shake by adding fruits such as bananas, strawberries, apricots and pineapple.

Maple Milk Shake

1 glass milk
2 scoops ice cream
2 T maple syrup

For each milk shake, blend or shake together.

Pies

Maple Meringue Pie

4 T cornstarch
¼ t salt
2 c milk
1⅓ c maple syrup

3 eggs, separated
1 T butter
1 t vanilla
1 9-inch baked pie shell

Beat egg yolks and set aside. Combine cornstarch and salt. Gradually add milk and 1 c maple syrup. Heat to boiling over direct heat and boil gently 1 minute, stirring constantly. Gradually add hot syrup mixture to beaten egg yolks. Return to medium heat and cook 2 minutes longer, stirring constantly. Add butter and vanilla. Mix thoroughly. Cool slightly; pour into baked pie shell. Beat egg whites until stiff but not dry. Gradually add remaining maple syrup to egg whites and continue beating until stiff. Spread meringue on top of filling, being careful to spread meringue to touch the crust at all points. Bake at 425°F for 4½ to 5 minutes or until lightly brown.

Maple Pecan Pie

1 unbaked pie shell	¾ c maple syrup
¼ c butter	3 eggs beaten until light
⅔ c firmly packed brown	1 c broken pecans
sugar	1 t vanilla
⅛ t salt	

Cream butter, brown sugar and salt. Stir in other ingredients. Turn into pie shell. Bake 10 minutes at 450°F, then turn heat down to 350°F. Bake 30 or 35 minutes longer. Serve with whipped cream or ice cream.

Maple Pecan Pie with Maple Meringue

Into a baked 9-inch pie crust pour the following:

2 T butter	Pinch of salt
¼ c flour	½ c water
1 c maple syrup	¾ c coarsely chopped
3 egg yolks	pecans
1 t vanilla	

Beat egg yolks until light and spongey. Add the flour, alternating with water. Add syrup, salt and vanilla and pour into a double boiler. Add the butter. Set the pan over heat and stir until custard is smooth and thick. Fold in the nuts and pour into baked pie crust. Top with:

Maple Meringue

3 egg whites
Pinch of salt
3 T maple syrup

Add salt to egg whites and beat until very stiff. Add syrup slowly. Spread over maple filling and roughen the surface. Put in a moderate oven (375°F) and bake until meringue browns— 15 to 20 minutes. Serve warm or cold.

Maple Pumpkin Pie

Pastry for pie
1½ c pumpkin
⅔ c brown sugar, packed
2 T maple syrup
½ t ginger
1 t cinnamon
¼ t cloves
½ t salt
2 eggs, beaten
1 c milk
½ c cream

Mix ingredients in the order given. Pour filling into pastry-lined pie pan and bake at 425°F for 10 minutes. Then reduce heat to 350°F and bake about 35 minutes or until done.

Maple Sugar Pie

Favorite pie pastry
3 eggs
3 T soft maple sugar
2 c milk
⅛ t nutmeg
½ t salt
½ t vanilla

Line pie pan with pastry and chill. Beat the eggs lightly and add the maple sugar. Heat milk in a double boiler, add nutmeg and salt and pour slowly over the eggs and sugar. Strain. Add the vanilla. Pour into pastry-lined pan and bake at 400°F until

Syrup Trees
by Bruce Thompson

Our Apologies —

CORRECTION
Please reverse maps on pages 4 and 8.

NOTE:
Many authorities, including Hortus III, consider sugar maple and black maple as variants of one species. Black maple is commonly found on calcareous soils and rarely occurs in New England.

the edge of the crust is lightly browned. Reduce the heat to 350°F and bake until knife inserted in filling comes out clean. Makes one 9-inch pie.

Puddings

Maple Nut Pudding

1½ c hot milk
2 eggs, separated and
    beaten
1 T gelatin
¼ c cold water
1 c maple syrup
¼ t salt
½ t vanilla
¼ c chopped nuts

Place hot milk and slightly beaten egg yolks in a double boiler. Cook over boiling water until the mixture coats a silver spoon. Stir constantly. Sprinkle gelatin on cold water and let stand 5 minutes. Add to hot mixture and stir until dissolved. Add the maple syrup and salt. Cool in refrigerator. When the mixture begins to congeal, fold in stiffly beaten egg whites, vanilla and nuts. Pour into serving glasses and chill. Serve with custard sauce.

Maple Syrup Bread Pudding

1 c maple syrup
1 c milk
2 c cubed, day-old
   bread

¼ t salt
2 eggs, beaten

Scald milk over hot water. Add maple syrup, bread and salt; let stand 5 minutes. Add beaten eggs and transfer to a well-greased casserole dish. Place in pan of hot water and bake in oven at 325°F for 60 minutes or until done.

Variations: ½ cup chopped nuts and ½ cup raisins may be added with the eggs.

Maple Syrup Pudding Sauce

¾ c maple syrup
¼ c water
½ c heavy cream,
   whipped

2 egg whites, stiffly
   beaten
1 t lemon juice

Boil maple syrup and water until mixture spins a thread, (228°F). Beat egg whites until stiff. Add syrup to egg whites gradually, beating constantly with an egg beater or at low speed on a mixer. Add lemon juice. Fold in whipped cream. Makes about 2 c.

Maple Tapioca Dessert

⅓ c instant tapioca
1 egg yolk, slightly
   beaten
1 c maple syrup
2 c milk, scalded

½ t salt
⅔ c nut meats
1 egg white, stiffly
   beaten

Combine tapioca, egg yolk, salt, maple syrup and milk; cook until tapioca is clear. Cool slightly. Fold in beaten egg white and nuts; chill.

Sauces and Glazes

Glaze for Ham

2½ c maple syrup	½ c apple juice
2 T mustard	½ pound fresh
½ c orange juice	cranberries
½ t cinnamon	1 T grated orange rind

Spread part of glaze on ham before last 30 minutes of baking, then the rest of glaze in 2 or 3 applications, about every 10 minutes.

Step One: Combine ½ c maple syrup, apple juice, mustard; pour over ham; baste occasionally.

Step Two: Cook cranberries with 1 c maple syrup until skins pop open. Press mixture through a sieve and spread over ham.

Step Three: Combine 1 cup maple syrup, orange juice and 1 T rind with cinnamon; mix well. Spread over ham.

Maple Sauce for Ham

¼ t salt	3 whole cloves
1 t mustard	1 c maple syrup
1 T cornstarch	

Mix dry ingredients in saucepan. Add maple syrup, stir and cook slowly until thickened and clear. Serve hot or cold.

Variations: Add ½ c crushed pineapple or ½ c cooked raisins to sauce.

Maple Sauce

½ c water	1 pound (2 c) maple
½ c walnut meats	sugar

Add the water to the maple sugar and boil until it reaches the thread stage (230°– 234°F). Add the walnut meats broken into small pieces. This sauce is good with ice cream, blanc mange or custard. It may be used hot or cold.

Vegetables

Maple Sweet Potatoes or Carrots

3 medium sweet potatoes or 1 bunch carrots (about 10)	¾ c maple syrup 2 T butter

Peel sweet potatoes or scrape carrots and cook in boiling water for 15 minutes. Drain; slice and arrange in buttered baking dish. Add syrup and butter and bake in a moderate oven (350°F) until tender and well-glazed, about 45 minutes, turning occasionally in syrup. Serves 6.

Maple Candied Sweet Potatoes

6 medium sweet potatoes	1 t salt
½ c maple syrup	1 c apple juice
1 T butter	½ c water

Boil potatoes in jackets until nearly tender. Peel and slice into baking dish. Heat remaining ingredients to boiling. Pour over potatoes and bake in slow oven (300°F) for 1 hour. Serves 6.

Maple Gingered Carrots

6 medium carrots	3 T butter
3 T maple syrup	½ t ginger

Slice carrots, cook until tender. Melt butter and combine with syrup and ginger. Simmer carrots in mixture until glazed.

Maple Baked Beans

Maple syrup is delicious on baked beans in place of other sweetening. Add the syrup to the beans before baking.

Meats

Maple Sausage and Apples

1 c pure maple or maple-blended syrup	1 pound pork sausage links
4 medium apples, cored and cut into ½″ rings	½ c distilled white vinegar

Fry sausage uncovered in large skillet over medium heat, turning occasionally, until golden brown—about 20 minutes. Drain sausage. Place on heated platter and keep warm. Meanwhile, mix maple syrup and vinegar in medium saucepan. Heat uncovered over medium heat to boiling; reduce heat. Stir in apple rings. Simmer uncovered over medium heat until apples are crisp-tender, about 5 minutes. Remove apple rings; arrange on platter with sausage. Pour syrup liquid over sausage and apples and serve immediately. Makes 4 servings.

Maple Syrup Ham

1 6–7 pound smoked ham	Baked sweet potatoes, halved
1 c pure maple or maple-blended syrup	1 quart apple juice
½ t dry mustard	⅓ c all-purpose flour
	1 c golden raisins

Heat ham, apple juice and syrup in 8-quart iron pot or Dutch oven over medium heat to boiling; reduce heat. Simmer covered 2½ hours. Remove ham from Dutch oven; trim outer skin from ham. Keep warm. Measure cooking liquid. Return 1 c of the cooking liquid to Dutch oven; reserve 3 c of the remaining liquid. Whisk flour and mustard into the liquid in Dutch oven. Cook over low heat, stirring constantly, until smooth. Add raisins and the reserved liquid to the flour mixture; cook, stirring constantly, until bubbly, about 10 minutes. Serve ham with sweet potatoes. Pass raisin sauce. Makes 10 servings.

Beverages

The unique ability of maple sugar to modify and smooth raw drinks has long been known, as illustrated by the following quotation from Carl Sandburg's *Abraham Lincoln.* "Following the wedding ceremony of Nancy Hanks to Thomas Lincoln in 1806, guests were invited to the 'infare.' One who was there remembered, 'We had bear meat, venison, wild turkey and ducks, eggs wild and tame, maple sugar lumps tied on a string to bite off for coffee or whisky, syrup in big gourds, peach and honey, a sheep barbecued whole over coals of wood burned in a pit, and covered with green boughs to keep the juices in; and a race for the whisky bottle.' "* Homemade

*Carl Sandburg, 1970, *Abraham Lincoln,* p. 18, The Readers Digest Association.

whisky, and even the 21-¢-a-pint storebought firewater, could well stand mellowing, and an accompanying bite of maple sugar was sorely needed to make it potable.

As for coffee, try a lump of maple sugar with it during the afternoon coffee break for a delicious, pleasant stimulant to see you through the rest of the day.

Experimental and Conjectural Recipes

I wish that I could give you an excellent recipe for maple wine, maple-fruit wine or brandy, but the closest I can come are the following taken from *How to Make Wines and Cordials* by André Simon.

Birch

The birch grows to perfection in the Highlands of Scotland, in Scandianavia, Russia and other northern lands where the vine does not thrive, and in the early spring of the year the birch may be tapped and its sap used for making a cordial wine.

Birch Wine
To every gallon of birch water, put 2 lb. of good sugar, boil it half an hour, skim it well, let it stand to settle, then pour it off from the sediment, and put yeast to it, and work it as you do ale 24 hours. Before you tun it, smoke your barrel with brimstone and to every gallon of liquor, put half a pound of slit raisins. Let it stand 3 or 4 months, then bottle it.

(MSS.H.101, late eighteenth century)

To Make Birch Wine
In March bore a hole in a birch-tree, and put in a faucet and it will run two or three days together without hurting the tree; then put in a pin to stop, and the next year you may draw as much from the same hole; put to every gallon of the liquor a quart of good honey and stir it well together; boil it an hour, skim it well, and put in a few cloves and a piece of lemon-peel when it is almost cold put

to it so much ale-yeast as will make it work like new ale; and when the yeast begins to settle, put it in a runlet that will just hold it; so let it stand six weeks, or longer if you please; then bottle it, and in a month you may drink it; it will keep a year or two; you may make it with sugar, two pounds to a gallon, or something more, if you keep it long; this is admirably wholesome as well as pleasant, an opener of obstructions, good against the phthisis, the spleen and scurvy, a remedy for the stone; it will abate heat in a fever or thrush, and has been given with good success.

(Gelleroy—London Cook 1762)

How to Make Birch Wine
The season for procuring the liquor from the birch-trees is in the beginning of March, while the sap is rising, and before the leaves shoot out, for when the sap is become forward and the leaves begin to appear, the juice, by being long digested in the bark, grows thick and coloured, which was before thin and clear.

The method of procuring the juice is, by boring holes in the body of the trees, and putting in faucets, which are commonly made of the branches of elder, the pitch being taken out; you may, without hurting the trees, if large, tap them in several places, four or five at a time, and by that means, from a good store of trees, save many gallons every day.

If you do not use it immediately, which is the best way, then in order to preserve it in a good condition for brewing, and that it may not turn sour till you have got the quantity you want, the bottle in which it dropped from the faucets, must be immediately well stopped, and the corks waxed or refined.

One method of making it is this, to every gallon of birch liquor put a quart of honey, stir them well together, put in a few cloves and a little lemon peel, and let it boil for near an hour, and scum it well continuously as the scum rises, then set it by to cool, and put in two or three spoonfuls of good ale yeast to set it working, and when the yeast begins to settle, put it in a runlet which will just hold it, and let it stand six weeks, or longer if you please, then bottle it; and it will be fit to drink in a month; it will keep good a year or two. If you have a mind to use sugar instead of honey, put two pounds to a gallon, or more if you would keep it long.

This wine is not only very wholesome, but pleasant; it is a most rich cordial, good in curing consumptions, phthisis, spleen, and also all such inward diseases as accompany the stone in the bladder. Dr. Needham says he has often cured the scurvy with the juice of birch boiled with honey and wine. It is also good to abate heart in a fever.

(The British Jewel 1782)

For Birch Wine
(As made in Sussex)
Take the sap branches, or the top of birch fresh cut, boil it as long as any scum arises; to every gallon of liquor put two pounds of sugar, boil it half an hour, and scum it very clean. When it is almost cold, set it with a little yeast, spread on a toast, ... let it stand five or six days in an open vessel, stirring it often; then take such a cask as the liquor will be sure to fill; fire three or four large matches dipped in brimstone and put it into the empty cask, and stop the cask till the match is extinguished, always keeping it shook or turned round; take out the ashes, and as quick as possible, pour into it a pint of sack or Rhenish, whichever taste you like best, for the liquor retains it; rinse the cask well with this and pour it out; pour in your wine and stop it close for six months, then if it is perfectly fine you may bottle it.

(Daily Companion 1799)

Sycamore Wine

To every gallon of the liquor fresh drawn from the tree, and boiled a quarter of an hour over the fire, add two pounds of the finest powdered sugar. Boil the liquor again for half an hour longer, taking off all the scum as it rises. When removed from the fire, and almost cold, barm it as you do birchwine; let it stand until it be white over, stirring it twice a day (viz. for three or four days), then smoke your barrel with a little brimstone; and when you tun it, put into each gallon of liquor one pound of Malaga raisins, clean picked and shredded (or a like quantity of loaf sugar), with the whites of two eggs. Stop it up close, and let it remain unmoved until the wine be perfectly fine, and then bottle it.

Note: That this sycamore wine, after it has stood a due time upon the raisins, is to be racked off into a clean cask, and depurated with isinglass, as directed in the making of birch-wine, if it be not then clear. You may gather the water or juice of the sycamore tree, for making this wine, in January.

(The Practical Distiller 1734)

To Make Sycamore Wine
Take two gallons of the sap and boil it half an hour, then add to it four pounds of the fine powder sugar, beat the whites of three eggs to a froth, and mix them with the liquor, but if it be too hot, it will poach the eggs, scum it very well, and boil it half an hour, then strain it through a hair sieve, and let it stand till next day, then pour it clean from the sediments, put half a pint of good yeast to every twelve gallons, cover it up close with blankets till it is white over, then put it into the barrel, and leave the bung-hole open till it has done working, then close it well up, let it stand three months, then bottle it, the fifth part of the sugar must be loaf, and if you like raisins, they are a great addition to the wine.

N.B. You may make birch wine the same way.

(English Housekeeper 1806)

A more recent recipe for Birch Wine is the following:

1 gallon birch sap	1 Campden Tablet
1 lb. raisins	1 t yeast nutrient
1½ lbs. sugar (use hydrometer starting specific gravity 1.090)	4 t acid blend
	¼ t grape tannin
	1 package wine yeast

Aging seems to be the *sine qua non* for excellent wine. A year in the bottle is recommended for most wines as a minimum. Accordingly, experienced wine makers make more than 1 gallon at a time, although this is an excellent experimental quantity.

Should you adapt the birch and sycamore recipes to maple to obtain maple wine, it can, of course, be converted to maple brandy simply by distilling the product. I have been told that a 60-proof maple brandy can be a most excellent and welcome addition to the cabinet of a connoisseur.

The action of bacteria on dilute solutions of ethyl alcohol derived from previous yeast fermentation can, incidentally, change the product to vinegar; as wine drinkers who leave their bottles uncorked have discovered.

Now if New England had been settled by drinkers of wine rather than drinkers of beer, if they had had a respectable wine yeast, if they had had cellars, if they had had no frontier to always beckon, and if rum, whisky, applejack and beer took as long to make as wine, the drinking habits of the country might be somewhat different. And we might have good maple wine recipes today. Wines have been imported since the early days of America, but they all came from countries which had no sugar maple. A substitute for unwholesome water made from pumpkins, maple sugar and persimmons was only temporarily in favor.

Theoretically, 1 pound of invert sugar is 0.51 pounds of absolute alcohol and 0.489 pounds of carbon dioxide. With selected yeasts, sugar can be made to yield 90% of the theoretical amount. 100 pounds of standard density maple syrup contains about 66.0 pounds of sugar—the actual amount may vary from 65 to 66.8 pounds. At 67 pounds, the syrup is supersaturated and the sugar will precipitate out when the solution is cooled.

I believe the amount of sugar in maple syrup is slightly higher than in the honey from which mead was formerly made in great quantities. The sugar content of maple sap is approximately the same as that of molasses, from which rum is made. The present cheapness of cane sugar and molasses obviously rules out making a similar end-product from maple, but if the energy situation really becomes desperate sometime down the line, remember that you can get alcohol from your maple trees.

Winemaking, whether from rhubarb, turnips, potatoes, grapes, sap or syrup, is inexpensive and easy. All major cities now have wine equipment supply stores, and most of them carry an assortment of books on proceedure. Here are a few you might look for:

Leigh P. Beadle, 1975, *Brew it Yourself,* Farrar, Straus and Giroux.
Ralph Auf der Heide, 1973,*The Illustrated Wine Book,* Doubleday and Company.
Bryan Acton and Peter Duncan, 1972, *Making Mead,* Standard Press.
Michael Barleycorn, 1976, *Moonshiners Manual,* Oliver Press/Charles Scribner's Sons.

The only other requirement is that you phone the Alcohol, Tobacco and Firearms division of the Internal Revenue Service and request Form 1541, fill it out and return it. Single persons or heads of a household not living with the family are ineligible. This permits you to make 200 gallons of wine for your own use. There is no charge, but the formality seems discriminatory and unnecessary. The hydrometer used in making maple syrup can be used in winemaking as well, and I suggest a modified mead called melomels for starters.

Now then . . . sit back, savor your food and drink, and happily reflect upon your independence and freedom . . . courtesy of the wonderful syrup trees.

11

Appendix

Research Notes

The Northeastern Forest Experiment Station of the Forest Service, 370 Reed Road, Broomall, Pennyslvania 19008, has published the results of various research projects conducted by the station and its branch at the Aiken Laboratory, P. O. Box 968, 705 Spear Street, Burlington, Vermont 05401. Included among them are:

> NE-61: "Controlling Taphole Depth in Maple Sap Production Research," M. R. Koelling and Baron M. Blum, 1967.
>
> NE-91: "Vacuum Pumping Doubles Maple Sap Yield on Flat Land," R. R. Morrow and C. B. Gibbs, 1969.
>
> NE-106: "Vacuum Pumping Increases Sap Yields from Sugar Maple Trees," Barton M. Blum and Melvin R. Koelling, 1968.
>
> NE-107: "Effect of Vacuum Pumping on Lateral Movement of Sap in the Maple Tree Hole," Barton M. Blum and Melvin R. Koelling, 1968.

NE-118: "Paraformaldehyde Pellet Not Necessary in Vacuum-Pumped Maple Sap System," Clay H. Smith and Carter B. Gibbs, 1970.

NE-126: "Tapping Near Old Tap Holes in Sugar Maple Trees," Clay H. Smith, 1971.

NE-134: "Maple Sugaring with Vacuum Pumping During the Fall Season," Clay H. Smith and Albert G. Snow, Jr., 1971.

NE-137: "Sap Volume as Influenced by Tubing Diameter and Slope Percent," Clay H. Smith, 1971.

NE-138: "Testing Sugar Maple Sap for Sweetness with a Refractometer," Clay H. Smith and George M. Keiser, 1971.

NE-141: "The Effect of Xylem Age on Volume Yield and Sugar Content of Sugar Maple Sap," Carter B. Gibbs, 1969.

NE-153: "The Relationship between Sap-Flow Rate and Sap Volume in Dormant Sugar Maples," W. J. Gabriel, R. S. Walters and D. W. Seegrist, 1972.

NE-155: "Cambial Dieback and Taphole Closure in Sugar Maple after Tapping," Carter B. Gibbs and Clay H. Smith, 1973.

NE-161: "Some Effects of Paraformaldehyde on Wood Surrounding Tapholes in Sugar Maple Trees," Alex L. Shigo and Frederick M. Laing, 1970.

NE-171: "A Guide to Sugar Bush Stocking," Clay H. Smith and Carter B. Gibbs, 1970.

NE-213: "Sugar Maple Sap Volume Increases as Vacuum Level is Increased," Clay H. Smith and Russell S. Walter, 1975.

NE-216: "Tubing vs. Buckets: A Cost Comparison," Neil K. Huyler, 1975.

NE-240: "Installing Plastic Tubing to Collect Maple Sap," Clay H. Smith and Albert G. Snow, Jr., 1972.

NE-286: "A Silvicultural Guide for Developing a Sugar Bush," Kenneth F. Lancaster, Russel S. Walters, Frederick M. Laing and Raymond T. Foulds, 1974.

NE-298: "Storage Requirements for Sugar Maple Seeds," H. W. Yawner and Clayton M. Carl, Jr., 1974.

NC-155: "Economic Values for Growth and Grade Changes of Sugar Maple in the Lake States," Richard M. Godman and Joseph J. Mendel, 1978.

HT-30: "How to Control Sapstreak Disease of Sugar Maple," Kenneth J. Kessler, Jr., 1978.

NOTE: Dr. F. Bryan Clark, director of the Northeastern Forest Experiment Station, is a dedicated professional eager to assist outside researchers with the entire resources of his office. I owe him a debt of gratitude for his assistance with this book and an earlier effort, *Black Walnut for Profit.*

NOTE: Photocopies of many helpful publications not listed here are also available from the University of Vermont. For a complete list, write to: Maple Research Laboratory, Marsh Life Science Building, University of Vermont, Burlington, Vermont 05401.

Papers
Highly informative and well-written papers such as the following may be obtained from the Extension Service, Cornell University, Ithaca, New York.

"Microbial Control in Sap Collection," R. R. Morrow, 1975.

"Tubing vs. Buckets for Maple Sap Collection," R. R. Morrow and J. Morse, 1975.

"Tree Crowns in Relation to Maple Sap Sugar Concentration," R. R. Morrow and D. Mudge, 1975.

"Tree Characteristics and Sap Flow," R. R. Morrow, 1975.

"The Cause of Maple Sap Flow," R. R. Morrow, T. Gajewski and A. Powers, 1975.

"Straight Talk on Tapping Techniques," R. R. Morrow and P. Worrall, 1975.

"Density of Sap and Sirup," R. W. Stefano and R. R. Morrow, 1976.

"Summary of Information of Packaging Sirup—Especially Plastic," R. R. Morrow, 1976.

Bulletins
"References Dealing with Maple Sap and Syrup Production and Use," Ralph D. Nyland, 1968. *AFRI Misc. Report No. 1,* State University, College of Forestry at Syracuse University, Syracuse, New York 13210 (lists 605 American and Canadian references by author and title through 1967).

"Production of Maple Sirup and Other Maple Products,"
F. E. Winch and R. R. Morrow, 1975. *Information
Bulletin 95,* Mailing Room, Building 7, Research
Park, Cornell University, Ithaca, New York 14853.

"Sugar Bush Management," R. R. Morrow, 1976. *Information Bulletin 110,* Mailing Room, Building 7, Research Park, Cornell University, Ithaca, New York
14853.

"Homemade Maple Syrup," M. R. Koelling and James E.
Neal, 1976. *Extension Bulletin 703,* Michigan State
University, East Lansing, Michigan.

"Characteristics and Attitudes of Michigan's Maple Syrup
Producers," J. E. Gunter and M. R. Koelling, 1975.
Research Report 257, Michigan State University, East
Lansing, Michigan.

"Maple Syrup Production in Michigan's Lower Penin-
sula," R. D. Nyland and V. J. Rudolph, 1970. *Research Report 106,* Michigan State University, East
Lansing, Michigan.

"Mini-Production of Maple Syrup," William Cowen, Jr.,
and Wilbur A. Gould. Cooperative Extension Service, The Ohio State University.

"Maple Sap Production Economics in Michigan," John E.
Gunter and M. R. Koelling, 1975. *Research Report
274,* Michigan State University, East Lansing,
Michigan.

"So You Want to Farm," T. G. Brown, 1977. *Agr. Econ. 3,*
Columbia Extension Division, University of Missouri.

"The Farm Woodlot," 1974. Ministry of Natural Resources, Forest Management Branch, Toronto, Ontario, Canada.

"The Forest Trees of Ontario," J. H. White (revised by
R. C. Hosie), 1975. Ministry of Natural Resources,
Toronto, Ontario, Canada.

"Sugar Bush Management for Maple Syrup Producers,"
C. F. Coons, 1976. Information Branch, Ontario
Ministry of Natural Resources, Parliament Building,
Toronto, Ontario M7A 1W3, Canada.

"Profitable Tapping of Sugar Maples in Michigan's Lower
Pennisula," R. D. Nyland and V. J. Rudolph, 1969.
Research Report 81, Michigan State University, East
Lansing, Michigan.

"Hardwood Trees of Ontario," E. J. Zavitz, 1973. Ministry of Natural Resources, Toronto, Ontario, Canada.

"Sugar Bush Management," R. R. Morrow, 1976. *Information Bulletin 110,* Mailing Room, Building 7, Research Park, Cornell University, Ithaca, New York 14853.

"Influence of Tapping Techniques on Maple Sap Yields," Putman W. Robbins. *Research Report 28,* Michigan State University, East Lansing, Michigan.

Technical bulletins and data on reverse osmosis as an aid or supplement to evaporation were supplied to me by Osmonics, Inc., 15404 Industrial Park Road, Hopkins, Minnesota 55343. Larger producers should familiarize themselves with the reverse osmosis procedure.

Periodicals

American Forests, American Forestry Association, 1319 Eighteenth St. N.W., Washington, D.C. 20036

American Nurseryman, American Nurseryman Publishing Co., 310 S. Michigan Ave., Chicago, Illinois 60604 (a source for seeds, seedlings, and useful material as well as informative articles)

Connecticut Woodlands, 1010 Main Street, P.O. Box 369, East Hartford, Connecticut 06108

Forest Farmer, P.O. Box 95385, Atlanta, Georgia 30347 (a grassroots organization of timberland owners—large and small—with active members in virtually every timbered county in the South)

National Maple Syrup Digest, published quarterly by Lloyd H. Sipple, R.D. #2, Bainbridge, New York 13733 (back copies may be available)

Ohio Woodlands, The Neil House, Columbus, Ohio 43215

Pennsylvania Forests, 5221 E. Simpson St., Mechanicsburg, Pennsylvania 17055

Trees—The Journal of American Arboriculture, 7621 Lewis R., Olmstead Falls, Ohio 44138

Virginia Forestry Association, 1 N. Fifth St., Richmond, Virginia 23219

Western Fruit Grower, Meister Publishing Company, 37841 Euclid Ave., Willoughby, Ohio 44094 (contains current information about developments on nut and fruit trees which is applicable to sugar trees also)

For specialized reading, timber producers may find items of interest in:

Directory of Forest Products Industry, Miller Freeman Publishers, Inc. 500 Howard St., San Francisco, California 94105

Journal of Forestry, 5400 Grosvenor Lane, Bethesda, Maryland 20014

National Hardwood Magazine, P.O. Box 18436, Memphis, Tennessee 38118

Plymouth Forest Industry Review, 170 Broadway, New York, New York 10038

Plywood and Panel Magazine, P.O. Box 567B, Indianapolis, Indiana 42606

Timber Tax Journal, International Scholarly Book Services, Inc., P.O. Box 555, Forest Grove, Oregon 97116

Wood and Wood Products, 300 W. Adams St., Chicago, Illinois 60606

The Woodbook, P.O. Box 1752, Tacoma, Washington 98401 (a 232-page catalog of product information and design data for all types of wood products)

Woodworking and Furniture Digest, Hitchcock Building, Wheaton, Illinois 60187

Publications in allied fields:

Nutshell, Northern Nut Growers Association, Dr. D. K. Ourecky, secretary; New York Experiment Station, Geneva, New York 14456

Small Woodland Owners Association of Main, R.R. 1, Pittsfield, Maine 04967 (write for a list of publications)

Song News, Society of Ontario Nut Growers, R. D. Campbell, ed.; R.R. 1, Niagara-on-the-Lake, Ontario, Canada Los 1JO

Occasional articles on maple syrup production may be found in many other magazines, such as *Harrowsmith, Country Gentlemen, Natural Life, Countryside, Mother Earth News, Organic Gardening* and *Farm Wife News.*

Books

Annual Report of the American Institute, No. 133, State of New York, 1853.

Michigan Trees, C. H. Otis, The University of Michigan Press, 1915.

World Geography of Forest Resources, Sayden-Guest, Wright, Teclaff, eds., American Geographical Society, Roland Press 1956.

Knowing Your Trees, G. H. Collinwood and Warren D. Brush, The American Forestry Association, Washington, D.C., 1964 (revised by Devereaus Butcher).

Atlas of United States Trees, Vol. 1, E. L. Little, Jr., Misc. Pub. 1146, U.S. Department of Agriculture, Washington, D. C., 1971.

Agricultural Handbook No. 134, C. O. Willits and C. H. Hills, Superintendent of Documents, U.S. Government Printing Office, Washington, D.C. 20402, 1976 (rev. ed.).

Amateur Sugar Making, Noel Perrin, University Press of New England, Hanover, New Hampshire.

The Maple Sugar Book, Helen and Scott Nearing, John Day Co., 1950.

Related References

Beet-Sugar Technology, R. A. McGinnis, Reinhold Publishing Co., 1951.

The Sugar Cane, A. C. Barnes, Interscience Publishers, Inc., 1964.

Cane Sugar Refining in the United States, Robert G. Nathan, Associates, U.S. Cane Sugar Refiners Association, Washington, D.C., 1971.

Also see "Sweet Tooth," Dana Sobell, *Harvard Magazine,* March–April 1978, p. 19.

Organizations

International Maple Syrup Institute
P.O. Box 220
Montreal, Canada H3Z 2T2

North American Maple Syrup Council
Garden Gowen, Secretary
Alstead, New Hampshire 03602

Ontario Maple Producers Association
1200 Bay Street, 9th Floor
Toronto, Ontario, Canada M7A 2B2

State organizations—inquire of the Agricultural Extension
Service in your state.

Comparison of Average Sap Flow of Sugar Maple and Soft Maple

This chart from Forest Service Report NE-286 is arranged by
diameter classes on the basis of number of buckets per tree for
both sugar and soft maple. The data was taken in Somerset
County, Pennsylvania, in 1931.

Diameter class	Average number of buckets hung	Sugar maple	Soft maple
		Average flow	Average flow
Inches	*No.*	*Quarts**	*Quarts**
9-16	1.0	8.9	5.5
17-23	1.5	15.1	7.4
24-28	2.2	17.7	12.5
29-33	2.8	22.4	13.4
34-36	3.6	27.7	20.3
37-45	3.8	31.7	18.9

*Short-term sap flow, not seasonal flow.

Number of Trees Required to Yield One Cord

The following table, extracted from University of Maine Bulletin #148, will help you estimate the number of cords of pulpwood (1 cord is 128 cubic feet) in a stand containing trees of various sizes. Diameters given are measured 4½ feet above the ground and outside the bark.

Diameter of Trees (inches)	Hardwood (Deciduous)	Softwood (Coniferous)
5	35	—
6	20	—
7	15	20
8	11	13
9	8	10
10	6	8
11	5	7
12	4	6
13	3.5	4.5
14	3.0	3.7
15	2.5	3.0
16	2.0	2.5
17	1.7	2.1
18	1.5	1.9
19	1.3	1.6
20	1.2	1.5
21	1.0	1.4
22	.9	1.2
23	.8	1.1
24	.7	1.0
25	.6	.9
26	.58	.8
27	.5	.77
28	.44	.7
29	.43	—

Index

Index of Recipes